PENGUIN BOOKS

SELECTED LETTERS OF JAMES THURBER

James Thurber was born in 1894 in Columbus, Ohio. After college he worked at the American Embassy in Paris from 1918 to 1920 and then turned to journalism. From 1927 he was on the staff of *The New Yorker* and first published much of his work in it. He died in 1961.

Helen Thurber, James Thurber's widow, now resides in Weston, Connecticut. After her husband's death Mrs. Thurber edited and published *Credos and Curios*, the book Thurber was working on at the time of his death, and *Thurber & Co.*, the last volume of Thurber's drawings.

Edward Weeks, Thurber's friend and his editor at *The Atlantic*, was editor of *The Atlantic* from 1938 to 1966. Since then he has been the Senior Editor and Consultant of the Atlantic Monthly Press. He is the author of eleven books; the most recent is *Writers and Friends*, a memoir.

D1057077

Books by James Thurber

‹‹•››

SELECTED LETTERS
◄ *of* ►
JAMES THURBER

Edited by

Helen Thurber &
Edward Weeks

PENGUIN BOOKS

Penguin Books Ltd, Harmondsworth,
Middlesex, England
Penguin Books, 625 Madison Avenue,
New York, New York 10022, U.S.A.
Penguin Books Australia Ltd, Ringwood,
Victoria, Australia
Penguin Books Canada Limited, 2801 John Street,
Markham, Ontario, Canada L3R 1B4
Penguin Books (N.Z.) Ltd, 182–190 Wairau Road,
Auckland 10, New Zealand

First published in the United States of America by
Little, Brown and Company, Inc., in association with the
Atlantic Monthly Press 1981
First published in Canada by
Little, Brown and Company (Canada) Limited 1981
First published in Great Britain by Hamish Hamilton Ltd 1982
Published in Penguin Books in the United States of America and Canada
by arrangement with Little, Brown and Company, Inc., in association
with the Atlantic Monthly Press
Published in Penguin Books 1982

LIBRARY OF CONGRESS CATALOGING IN PUBLICATION DATA
Thurber, James, 1894–1961.
Selected letters of James Thurber.
1. Thurber, James, 1894–1961—Correspondence.
2. Humorists, American—20th century—Correspondence.
I. Thurber, Helen.   II. Weeks, Edward, 1898–
III. Title.
[PS3539.H94Z48   1982]   818'.5209   [B]   82-9081
ISBN 0 14 00.6353 6   AACR2

Printed in the United States of America by
R. R. Donnelley & Sons, Harrisonburg, Virginia
Set in Palatino

The letter to Lewis Gannett and "A Birthday Poem for Lewis Gannett" are
reprinted by permission of the Houghton Library. The letters from John
O'Hara are reprinted by permission of the United States Trust Co. of New
York as Trustee under the will of John O'Hara; from Dr. Gordon Bruce by
permission of Dr. Bruce; from Charles Morton by permission of Cynthia
Morton Hollingsworth; to Harold Ross by permission of the Collection of
American Literature, Beinecke Rare Book and Manuscript Library, Yale
University. *The New Yorker*'s "Farewell" is reprinted by permission of
E. B. White and William Shawn.

A portion of this book appeared in *The Atlantic*.

Contents

✦

The Letters of James Thurber

◄◄►►

Adams was a great letter writer of the type that is now almost extinct
. . . his circle of friends was larger perhaps and more distinguished
than that of any other American of his generation.

— H. S. COMMAGER on *Letters of Henry Adams*

James Thurber was a letter writer of the type that is now completely
extinct. His circle of correspondents was perhaps no larger but it
was easily more bewildered than that of any other American of his
generation. Thurber laid the foundation for his voluminous correspondence during his Formative Period. In those years he wrote to
many distinguished persons, none of whom ever replied, among
them Admiral Schley, Young Barbarian, Senator Atlee Pomerene,
June Caprice, and a man named Unglaub who played first base for
the Washington Senators at the turn of the century. Unglaub, in
Thurber's estimation, stood head and shoulders above all the rest
of his correspondents and, indeed, he said so in his letter to Mc-
Kinley. Thurber did not write as many letters as Henry Adams or
John Jay Chapman or some of the other boys whose correspondence
has been published lately, but that is because he never set pen to
paper after his forty-third year.

The effect of Thurber's letters on his generation was about the
same as the effect of anybody's letters on any generation; that is to
say, nil. It is only when a man's letters are published after his death
that they have any effect and this effect is usually only on literary
critics. Nobody else ever reads a volume of letters and anybody
who says he does is a liar. A person may pick up a volume of cor-

respondence now and then and read a letter here and there, but he never gets any connected idea of what the man is trying to say and soon abandons the book for the poems of John Greenleaf Whittier. This is largely because every man whose letters have ever been published was in the habit of writing every third one to a Mrs. Cameron or a Mrs. Winslow or a Miss Betch, the confidante of a lifetime, with whom he shared any number of gaily obscure little secrets. These letters all read like this: "Dear Puttums: I love what you say about Mooey! It's so devastatingly true! B—— dropped in yesterday (Icky was out at the time) and gave some sort of report on Neddy but I am afraid I didn't listen (*ut ediendam aut debendo!*). He and Liddy are in Venice, I think I gathered, or Newport. What in the world do you suppose came over Buppa that Great Night? ? ? You, of course, were as splendidly consequent as ever (*in loco sporenti abadabba est*) — but I was deeply disappointed in Sig's reaction. All he can think of, poor fellow, is Margery's 'flight.' Remind me to tell you some day what Pet said about the Ordeal." These particular letters are sometimes further obscured by a series of explanatory editorial footnotes, such as "Probably Harry Boynton or his brother Norton," "A neighbor at Bar Harbor," "The late Edward J. Belcher," "Also sometimes lovingly referred to as Butty, a niece-in-law by his first marriage." In the end, as I say, one lays the book aside for "Snow-Bound" in order to get a feeling of reality before going to bed.

Thurber's letters from Europe during his long stay there in 1937 and 1938 (the European Phase) are perhaps the least interesting of all those he, or anybody else, ever wrote. He seems to have had at no time any idea at all, either clear or vague, as to what was going on. A certain Groping, to be sure, is discernible, but it doesn't appear to be toward anything. All this may have been due in great part to the fact that he took his automobile to Europe with him and spent most of his time worrying about running out of gas. The gasoline gauge of his car had got out of order and sometimes registered "empty" when the tank was half full and "full" when it contained only two or three gallons. A stronger character would have had the gauge fixed or carried a five-gallon can of *essence* in the back of the car, thus releasing the mind for more mature and significant preoccupations, but not Thurber.

Editors' Note

◄◄►►

The reader may wish to know a few of the preferences that governed our editing of these letters. Most obvious is our departure from the iron grip of chronology. In "The Thurber Circle," for instance, we begin with Wolcott Gibbs because, apart from E. B. White, he was Thurber's closest friend among the *New Yorker* contributors, and because the three striking letters to Gibbs tell more about their careers if they are read together than if they were interspersed chronologically throughout the section.

On the question of editorial interpolations and footnotes: we determined to use them as sparingly as possible, and often not at all if the general meaning is clear without a specific identification or explanation. In the cluster "Mr. Thurber Regrets," in which the writer declines some of the multitude of requests showered upon him, it is the grace and brevity of the refusal that matters, not the identity of the stranger asking the favor. Most of those letters are brief, and we wished them to be read spontaneously, not with a halter around the neck. In the final cluster to E. B. and Katharine White, where Thurber denounces the penny-pinching attitude of *New Yorker* editor Harold Ross toward the magazine's hard-pressed contributors, we decided that adding the full name of every writer or editor, some mentioned only in passing, would have resulted in a dusty cellar of footnotes. It seemed more sensible, for the most part, to let the context suffice and to place the full names in the index.

When the original letters were incompletely headed, we ascribed the apparent date and place of origin and put these letters in logical sequence, though we dispensed with the conventional practice of adding a clutter of brackets to emphasize the editing. Similarly, typographical errors, occasional misspellings, minor inconsistencies of style have been corrected. We wanted to avoid distracting the reader, while preserving the rhythm, the spoofing, the uncanny memory, the flight of imagination, and the affection with which Thurber wrote.

— HELEN THURBER AND EDWARD WEEKS

I have been unable to find any one of Thurber's many correspondents who saved any of his letters (Thurber himself kept car-
bons, although this is not generally known or cared about). "We
threw them out when we moved," people would tell me, or "We
gave them to the janitor's little boy." Thurber gradually became
aware of this on his return to America (the Final Phase) because of
the embarrassed silence that always greeted him when, at his
friends' homes, he would say, "Why don't we get out my letters to
you and read them aloud?" After a painful pause the subject was
quickly changed, usually by putting up the ping-pong table.

In his last years the once voluminous letter writer ceased writing
letters altogether, and such communication as he maintained with
the great figures of his time was over the telephone and consisted
of getting prominent persons on the phone, making a deplorable
sound with his lips, and hanging up. His continual but vain attempts to reach the former Barbara Hutton by phone clouded the
last years of his life but at the same time gave him something to
do. His last words, to his wife, at the fag end of the Final Phase,
were "Before they put up the ping-pong table, tell them I am not
running out of gas." He was as wrong, and as mixed up, in this
particular instance as he was in most others. I am not sure that we
should not judge him too harshly.

James Thurber

LETTERS FROM ABROAD
‹ *to* ›
E. B. WHITE AND KATHARINE

It was E. B. White who in February 1927 presented James Thurber to Harold Ross, editor of The New Yorker. *Ross assumed that White and Thurber were friends, although actually they had met only a few minutes earlier, and as Ross was continually in search of the ideal managing editor, he hired Thurber on the spot, at twice the salary Thurber had been receiving as a reporter for the* New York Evening Post.

For the ensuing six months Thurber and White shared the same office, and over the years their friendship was gloriously productive. They collaborated in the writing of their book Is Sex Necessary? *and White persuaded Eugene Saxton of Harper and Brothers to reproduce Thurber's drawings as, later, he persuaded Ross to accept them for* The New Yorker.

In the spring of 1936 Thurber wrote to White and his wife Katharine (a New Yorker *editor) from Bermuda, where he was relaxing with his second wife, Helen.*

Waterville Inn
Paget East, Bermuda
April 1936

Dear Katharine and Andy:

It was fine to get the little woman's letter today, which certainly contained a lot of news in two pages. It came in on the *Lafayette* this — Saturday — afternoon and we read it just before dinner. I wouldn't have been able to read it earlier because last night we started with Manhattans at our little cottage and then went dancing at the Bermudiana with Ronald and Jane Williams, two lovely youngsters I met when I visited the Sayres here.[1] He edits *The Bermudian* magazine. Jane is one of the world's prettiest girls (Helen says I kept telling Jane last night she was *the* world's most beautiful girl). We sat up all night and drank Scotch — the first time we have misbehaved really. Then today we had tea as our first meal at a nice place on the water front called the Little Green Door. Nothing in

1. Joel Sayre, a writer for *Time* and *The New Yorker*, and his wife Gertrude.

my life has ever tasted finer than the strawberries and cream and tea and toast. I shall remember it all my life — we were virtually starved, having missed breakfast and lunch at Waterville (Water Lock Inn is a new place up near Gibbs lighthouse). . . .

Ronnie Williams, by the way, has one great desire and that is to meet Andy. He thinks Andy's Comment[2] is the most consistently fine column of writing in the civilized world (which it is). Andy would like him greatly. He went to sea when he was sixteen, sailed before the mast, became an officer, was at it six years. He is, like Andy, a great lover of sailing boats, and an expert. Wants to go sailing here with Andy. He's English, but nice English. The Williàmses — he's twenty-eight and she twenty-three — are the sought after people down here. They usually have a writer in their home, which is tough, but they like it. Sinclair Lewis is one of their great admirers and we all went to dinner with him one night. Your dinner with him, my sweets, was nothing. Nothing. I'll tell you about it later. We decided, though, that he would be quite a swell guy sober. Maybe because he can, and did, recite most of *The Owl in the Attic.* The only drunken writer I ever met who said nothing about his own work and praised that of another writer present. He was poured onto the boat that took him home. He did one swell thing: he brought down here the eighty-three-year-old mother of his secretary, paid her way for two weeks in fine style. She was a wonderful old lady who had never been out of Rutland, Vt., before. Lewis went into a church with her, and knelt down when she did (and he brags about being the world's leading atheist). He was extremely fine with her and I liked him for it. . . .

We like our little cottage on the hill among the cedars very much. . . . Ada[3] has a tennis court, on which we played ten sets in two days, me cursing every second stroke, for I never played before. I got five games in the ten sets by some miscues. Down here, by the way, you might tell Moffat,[4] his "Finals at Lost Lake" is considered the funniest thing we ever printed. It was a grand piece of humor. . . . It is hard for me to realize I just can't walk up

2. "Notes and Comment," which traditionally began *The New Yorker*'s "Talk of the Town" section.

3. Ada Trimingham, owner and hostess of the Waterville Inn.

4. Donald Motiat, regular contributor to *The New Yorker.*

to the service line and serve like Stoefen.[5] I have the height and the reach for it. My measurements are almost identical with Vines's.[6] But never having played before, I couldn't do it. However, I am much better every time I play. Helen is really very good, although she hasn't played for ten years. She used to win cups and things. She trimmed the panties off papa, too. Once in a while I got in a fine forehand drive down the line. But in making a backhand I look and act like a woman up under whose skirts a bee has climbed. I will get over this. I must get over it. . . .

Give my best regards to everybody, and kiss Ross. He is, as my mother said, a mighty splendid man and, as his mother said, I hope someday he will become connected with *The Saturday Evening Post.* He deserves a future and I think he will go far.

> *Special love to you both,*
> *from both of us,*
>
> JIM & HELEN . . .

Sunday:

I got to four-games-all with Helen today, but she was not to be denied, as the sportswriters say, and ran out the set and the next nine games. She was way off form.

5. Lester Stoefen, U.S. men's doubles champion, 1933 and 1934.
6. H. Ellsworth Vines, 1932 men's singles winner at Wimbledon.

P.S. A letter from Gert Sayre (in Hollywood). I quote: "Professor Willie Strunk[7] is now here as technical adviser to *Romeo and Juliet* and doing nicely, thank you, you can tell Andy. Ah, my favorite artist, said the Professor, seeing our Thurber on the wall; he is, said the Professor, the American Utamaro.[8] I have tried to find out from my erudite friends who Utamaro is and how you spell it but they don't know either. Do you? . . . It is queer to see Willie, once the voice of authority in English-8, being quite wide-eyed and humble in Hollywood. He adores gazing upon Harlow and Shearer — who wouldn't? But he doesn't even seem to mind gazing on Sam Marx and Thalberg."

I think maybe Willie meant the American Untermeyer, although which one I don't know.

---

7. William Strunk, Jr., White's friend and English teacher at Cornell University, and author of *The Elements of Style* (which White revised in later years).
8. Kitagawa Utamaro, Japanese graphic artist.

In 1937 the Thurbers were living temporarily in Europe on the sale of his drawings, which had been exhibited in London. White was in a fallow period, and Thurber was incensed that he should be writing for The Saturday Evening Post.

◄◄◊►►

London, England
1937

Dear Andy:

As far as I can make out, what you have is sheep blast. It comes from an admixture of Comment writing and whisk broom catchings. You look up under "blast" in the dictionary. It is really a flatulent condition of certain sheep, and this is unusual because sheep have almost no diseases. You couldn't give a sheep syphilis, for instance, or vent gleet. Sheep bleat, of course, is common enough, and I have it myself. It causes one to say, "Hello, George," to himself in the mirror of a morning. Over here everybody turns Catholic when anything is the matter, and perhaps you should try that. T. S. Eliot turned Catholic and so did Evelyn Waugh and they look fine.

Your letter was appreciated in this far land, for no *New Yorker* mail ever reaches us. I sent in a casual[1] June 15 or so, where it was met with a stubborn silence, although I heard from a later casual and an earlier one. I'm sure they didn't buy it, but I'd like that it should be mentioned what happened, for you could hear a bomb drop I wait so quietly. Ross sent a note saying a check had been deposited for my last casual but Ralph Paladino[2] is dead and I never hear from his estate as to what has been deposited.

Fortunately, I have been selling drawings over here and we live very nicely on that. *Night and Day*, the London imitation of *The New Yorker*, bought a flock of rejected drawings yesterday, which Miss Terry[3] shipped me, and when they are printed there will be a

1. The staff's term for essay or short story.
2. Ross's assistant.
3. Daise Terry, office manager at *The New Yorker*.

Black Doubt: Is his wife out with an old beau?

hell of a kick from the Art Conference [at *The New Yorker*], which will not remember ever having seen them. The only drawings they remember vaguely are the ones I send in three or four times until they are bought to shut me up. *Night and Day* bought "The Patient" series, which I did in Bermuda and which you liked, but nobody else liked but me — nine drawings of a guy in bed. The Art Conf. dropped them like a mechanical match box. When I told *Night and Day* that you and I liked them, they said fine.

You are held in considerable awe over here for your Comment, Newsbreaks, verse, captions, and dizzy spells, but also because every piece ever printed about my drawings relates how you discovered them and stuffed them down the throats of Saxton, Hartman[4] and Ross, and me. . . .

Helen and I got the car out for the first time since my memorable advent in London, and drove to a beauty spot in Hampshire sixty

4. Lee Hartman, editor of *Harper's* magazine.

miles from London, on the old Southampton road, now the new Southampton road. Three or four couples who are painters, writers, editors, rented a great estate there with thirty rooms, tennis court, bowling green, *boule* court, etc., for $45 a month. We had a swell time, for they are all very nice people. Our contacts with the English have been very nice and maybe we've been lucky. We're going this weekend to a place near Kenilworth to visit a guy I went to Ohio State with, who assures me in a note that he hates the guts of all English. His letter came in the same mail with one from Miss Dawes, who used to be Ingersoll's[5] secretary, asking me did I remember the time I threw an alarm clock out of Mac's window onto 45th Street. She lives in Bath or Flinders Bottom, or Horsey Rinse. I think she has ferret bite. . . .

You would have been interested in a Bentley two-seater that one of the men had down in Hampshire. It's ten years old (1927 model), all black, long and narrow, with the handbrake on the outside of the door and right next to the handbrake, also on the outside, another lever which tilts your headlights up or down. The running board is set six inches away from the body to give play to this mechanism. The gear shift, amazingly enough on the inside of the car, is eight inches high, and works with a minimum of effort in a minimum of space. It never gets caught in anyone's knee or crotch. The seat is swung low, but is erect, and the car so made you have a clear view all around.

The English don't drive as fast as the French but they take just as big chances, passing on curves, blind corners, up grades, etc., with only a tenth of a second to make it in. I think the American drivers are, on the average, better than any. It is our garage mechanics, men in their forties who have been unsuccessful in love and got drunk, and youths in their twenties who have been successful in love and got drunk, who crack into things back home, together with college professors eighty years old who forget they are driving, but over here everybody drives like that. If you haven't got your license yet in England your car bears a big red *L* for learner, but you can't tell the difference in the driving. I am really the cat's arm when it

---

5. Ralph McAllister Ingersoll, managing editor of *The New Yorker* from 1925 to 1930.

comes to driving, and going on the left you soon get onto, although it's a little bad having a left-hand drive in England. Most Continental countries drive our way. . . .

Let me know more about whatever goes on. And be sure and get tested for sheep blast. Helen joins me in sending our love to you and Katharine and all the children, dogs, and turkeys. Look out for turkey wart, which catches you in the nerves and kidneys.

As ever,

J*IM*

◄◄►►

Paris, France
October 6, 1937

Dear Andy:

You may be a writer in farmer's clothing but you are still a writer. You are a writer and go about saying you are not a writer. . . .

In the October *Atlantic* Wilson Follett deplores the annihilation of the sentence in one place, while Gertrude Stein drops bombs on the sentence in another place. Every man must make his choice: you are either for Stein or for Follett. This is not a time for writers to escape to their sailboats and their farms. What we need is writers who deal with the individual plight and who at the same time do not believe in [Walter] Lippmann. It came to me today, walking in the rain to get Helen a glass of orange juice, that the world exists only in my consciousness (whether as a reality or as an illusion the evening papers do not say, but my guess is reality). The only possible way the world could be destroyed, it came to me, was through the destruction of my consciousness. This proves the superiority of the individual to any and all forms of collectivism. I could enlarge on that, only I have what the French call "rheumatism of the brain" — that is, the common cold.

David Garnett has come out with the quiet announcement that I am the most original writer living, but I have no clean handkerchiefs and the linge is not due till tomorrow. I started to make a list of all writers living but the names blurred on me. Of course, if you are no longer a living writer you don't belong in the list, which ought to cheer you up. Garnett goes on to say that in one miserable place I sound like Mark Twain talking from the grave, which ought to cheer you up, too. (This is where I say that I don't believe in scientists.) He thinks I ought to give up ideas and institutions, which I have long suspected, as after a great deal of study of them I feel that I do not know anything at all about them. This leaves me with only the dog and the wood duck and my own short-sighted blundering into other people's apartments and tulip beds, to deal with. Which is just as well. Garnett points out that Twain ended up by telling everybody there is nothing at all in art and music, in the aesthetic in general, and I guess he feels I will end up by telling everybody there is nothing in science, whether natural, organic, inorganic, or Freudian. It's high time I shut my trap and was reminded of the time my father got locked in the men's room on his wedding night. Well, his warning came just in time (Garnett's), for I have been on the verge of saying there was nothing in collectivism or in Lippmann's denunciation of it, either, and one more step from there and you are in Twain's grave. . . .

Helen has been in bed in our red room (everything in the room is red) for three days, and I have established a remarkable relationship with a waiter at the Café de Flore on the corner. This café is one of the few places in France which makes orange juice the way Helen wants it: pressed out of fresh oranges, strained, served with ice. Last night I went there to explain in my unusual French that I wanted a glass of orange juice to take to my sick wife in the Hôtel Crystal just around the corner. The waiter wanted to sell me orange juice that comes in a bottle, but I said I had to have it in a glass. So everybody in the café got in on it and finally the patronne of the café said all right, if I paid a deposit of three francs on the glass. So I did that. Then next time I borrowed a glass from the hotel and, taking the café's glass back, explained that now they could keep their glass and give me the three francs and put the fresh orange juice in this, my own glass. Helen said I would never be able to work that, and she was right.

There was a discussion in French, English, American, and gestures, about this, and although I got my idea over, it was flatly rejected. All the waiters got in on it, as well as the patronne, the gérant, the patron, his sister, a dishwasher, and two Frenchmen who were sitting in a corner. It was decided that the orange juice should again be put in the café glass which I had brought back and that the hotel glass should be returned to me, which it was. I have made several trips since then, taking the café glass back and having it filled up again. I'm going to try to work in the hotel glass again in a few days when things quiet down, and although I don't expect to get away with it, it is all very good practice in speaking French and in understanding the French people. . . . It is things like this, small, intense, unimportant, crucial, that make life in France a rich experience. . . . I may do a piece on the hotel glass, which may

Left Bank Hotel
(*The elevator of the Thurbers' hotel on the Left Bank was on the outside of the building and rarely, if ever, worked after midnight. This is Helen and Jamie returning to their room at two o'clock in the morning.*)

well make Garnett believe that not only Twain but Whitman is speaking from his grave.

You are not the writer who should think that he is not a writer. Let [James Branch] Cabell do that. Why doesn't Cabell decide he is not a writer? Why does Hervey Allen go on thinking he is a writer? What makes [Bernard] De Voto put down so many words? H. G. Wells has got the idea he is three or four writers. Meanwhile the bacteria are working quietly away. The sheep tick in England has just about got sheep and man, too, where he wants it. And forty thousand of them don't have to drill with spades all at once, either. The sheep tick knows what he is doing. Up in Warsaw, owls attacked an old woman who was just walking along. Owls know what they are doing, too. . . . Ah, well.

As ever,

JIM

◄◄◆►►

Cap d'Antibes, France
January 20, 1938

Dear Andy:

I agree, as usual, with all your sound conclusions about things except the one about not being able to escape from beaten states by merely taking a boat and watching somebody balance a 20-gallon water jar on her head. That is, it seems to me, the only way to escape from such things. . . .

I felt I could not leave New York and my trips to Cambridge and my nervous overnight post looking toward Columbus, where hell of one kind or another pops every few minutes, or did. But my daughter[1] and I have established a new and strong tie; we engage in a fine and remarkable correspondence, notable for her ability to say everything that is necessary in two sentences without punctuation and my own surprising ability to write that hardest of all things, a letter to a girl six years old. My family seems to have taken on new courage and strength now that I am away; my mother's letters, while no funnier, are more cheerful, . . . my father is doing all right. . . . I had worried a lot about being away a year, came close to abandoning the idea as being impossible, and then saw that because of as well as in spite of my fussing about it, I'd have to go. You got to get away where you can see yourself and everybody else. I really believe you got to do that. A week at Foord's [sanatorium], quick trips to Maine, a month on the wagon, are no good.

. . . It is almost impossible to have any faith at all in the adult male in these days: he continues to boggle everything as he always has boggled it. But because he is doing this I see no reason to go to pieces personally. I see every reason not to. I don't think the barricades is an answer, nor giving up appreciation of and interest in such fine, pleasant, and funny things as may still be around. A couple of Englishmen have written books recently saying that the better minds, the finer souls, the nobler spirits, should kind of go into

---

1. Rosemary, Thurber's only child, born to Althea, his first wife, in 1931.

a monastery, form a group on the old pattern of the monks, and see if that wouldn't help. Everybody wants to do something strange, and is.

It remains for a few people to stand and watch them and report what it all looks like and sounds like. Among such persons there isn't anybody better qualified for the job than you. If you will quit sending pieces to *The Saturday Evening Post.* I have pondered all day about you sending the Memoirs of a Master there. What was the matter with that excellent weekly called *The New Yorker?* It is important that things like Memoirs of a Master be printed and continue to be printed. . . . I wish you would explain to me what all this *Post* business is, anyway. That's not your audience. *Harper's, Scribner's,* the *Forum,* maybe, if you must get outside *The New Yorker,* but not the *Post.* The piece you did for them last year was the best piece they ever had and the best written they ever had, and probably thousands of readers wrote in to complain about that. Of course, it is my carefully arrived at and calmly studied opinion that *The New Yorker* is the best magazine in the world. I think that, of such intelligent people as there are, most of them read *The New Yorker.* More than read anything else. There is, on the other hand, I imagine, nobody of any importance at all in the United States of America who reads *The Saturday Evening Post.*

Of course, it does no good to reason with you in these matters, but still I keep on trying. I not only feel, but know as a fact, that anyone who can write the way you do has to keep on writing. I don't mean any crap about the Urge or anything like that. I mean it is a point of moral necessity. It seems to be easy for you to rationalize, deprecate, and dismiss this, but I don't think it will really work. Like tucking sex in the back of your mind and saying well, that's *that*. . . .

It was funny to get your letter and one from the Coateses[2] in the same mail, you talking about giving up your town house and life and moving to the country, they talking about selling their country place and moving to the city; both of you uncertain as to whether you can, or ought to. You two families ought to get together and compare notes. We are all against their selling their country place.

2. Robert M. Coates, novelist and short-story writer, was best man when Thurber married Helen; his wife Elsa was a bridesmaid.

"When I wore a tulip . . ."

They have got to the city after too long a time at a stretch in the country and have fallen under the city's spell — a pretty strong one at first — but in a year or so they would be exactly where you are, only they wouldn't have a home they own to go to. I think you should firmly argue them out of selling the country place. I am going to scream against it.

The New York life will get them sooner or later, probably sooner, as it gets everybody. I don't mean "city life," I mean New York City life, two different things. There is nothing else in all the countries of the world like New York City life. It does more to people, it socks them harder, than life in Paris, London, or Rome, say, possibly could. Just why this is I have been very interested in pondering over here. I know it is a fact, but I am not sure just why it is. Perhaps [Wolcott] Gibbs gets close to it in the Comment of January 8th when he speaks, rather more easily and naturally than bitterly, of "our horrible bunch." He means, of course, their horrible life. And God knows it sometimes is. People have to run away from it, broken or screaming, at the loveliest times of year, on fete days, just before parties, on Christmas Eve. . . .

I know I never want to live in it again for long at a time, just run down for a visit now and then. God knows it got me. I was the leader of those it got. This seems remarkable to me, now, from

here. I can see that tall, wild-eyed son of a bitch, with hair in his
eyes, and a glass in his hand, screaming and vilifying, and it's hard
for me to recognize him. I know that I will never let him get on the
loose again. I also know that a steady life in New York would do it.
Oddly enough, I don't think this is due to weakness, any more than
having your leg carried away by a shell is due to weakness. A city
made of steel and cement, with very few trees, and such trees as
there are, paltry and vulgar, sad and almost sordid, a city in which
it is possible to live for weeks and move around for miles without
seeing green grass and blue sky and never to hear crickets or frogs
or silence can have the same unavoidable effect as a shell from a
gun. The men who studied the effect on the minds of soldiers of
living in devastated areas, such as those around Verdun, came to
the conclusion that it did horrible things to them and that this cannot be avoided in places where there is no green and blue, no birds
and no animals and no insects. New York is nothing but a peace-
able Verdun, with music and the theatre — the only things that keep
people as sane as they are.

Liquor, of course, tends to keep people away from music and the
theatre. Bleeck's,[3] when you analyze it, is very much like a front-
line dug-out — the noise, the dogged courage of the men holding
on till zero hour, the fits of hysteria, the sitting around in sullen
gloom. The women are like the shattered trees of Verdun or the
shells whistling overhead. A place like Bleeck's would be impossible, I think, in Paris, Rome, London, Vienna. To see Villa Borghese,
Berkeley Square, the Bois de Boulogne, is to realize that Central
Park with its grim mall, its brave trees, its iron and cement closing
in on all sides, is merely an extension of Bleeck's offering no liquor.
A person can admire New York and so on, and all that, but I feel it
is absolutely impossible to love the place. One more or less holds
on there. It is an achievement to have lived there, not a pleasure to
do so. It has to be seen now and again, visited, lived in for short
periods, but I swear that all the laws of nature and of the constitu-
tion of man make it imperative not to live there. Not, at least, in
our horrible bunch. Something, I suppose, could be done about the
dreary, fatiguing, and maniac parties, although it is a little late.

3. A bar in New York's West Forties much frequented by journalists.

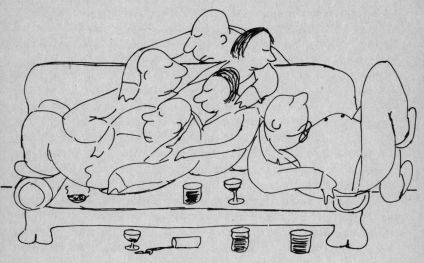

Four O'Clock in the Morning

They could be given up completely for a while. Why is it that people go on the wagon instead of giving up all intercourse? It may be the intercourse rather than the liquor, although I think it is both.

The cocktail parties at which it is obviously impossible to have any fun at all look very strange and wonderful from here. I keep telling people about them; nobody believes me. They no longer sound real to me as I tell them: everybody slugged or sick at a quarter to seven, holding on without dinner until 10:45, going home to sleep in a draught with one's hat on and a cold hamburger sandwich in one hand, rousing up at twelve to vomit and call somebody up and say you're sorry and to hear him shout at his wife to shut up, it's just Bert calling back. I say nobody believes it, and I am beginning to doubt it myself. And then back to bed, without quite getting your pants off, and the bell rings and it's Harry and Ella, he sick all over his Christmas scarf, she wanting to go on to Harlem. And wonderful stories of how Louise let everything burn or get cold so she and Jack didn't get any dinner at all, and how they left Merton asleep under the piano, and the whole crowd went over to Spitty's on Third Avenue for steaks but didn't eat them when they were brought. And Mike finally got Bill told off about his wife and she screamed that she loved Mike and Bill just sat down and cried, only on the overturned chair, so Mike stayed on and Greta made scrambled eggs for all three of them.

This thing is running on and on. I got to get to bed. I'm sorry as hell you are going to miss the sweet life that revolves around the little villa. It's terribly nice, my boy, with the rosemary in bloom and the fragrance of the mimosa trees coming in your room like rain when you open the windows, and sunsets such as nobody ever saw before, and Maria's chats about the political situation and life in general just before she leaves us for the night, after serving the coffee, and a great peace and quiet all over everything (and bottles of Scotch and rye and brandy untouched upstairs for weeks, await-ing the arrival of Miss Flanner[4] and our bi-monthly party). We would like like hell to buy this villa, which is for sale for about $5000 — it rents in the summer, when we wouldn't be here, for enough to pay back the purchase price in ten years.

Well, let me hear from you.

Love to you all, from us both,

J<small>IM</small>

P.S. I finished all the foregoing off last night after midnight and here it is three o'clock of a fine summer, or maybe spring, after-noon. I can see, in this new light, that your problem about the city house is not so easy. What's the matter with renewing the lease and kind of living there half the time, Maine the other half? Or anyway, your three months in Maine (make it four). Eight months in New York, with visits to the Thurbers in Connecticut is bearable, and anyway you like New York and except for walking into cars you don't let it get you so much. I also think you should go back to Comment, without letting it depress or kill you, because it was the best column in the country and something to find satisfaction in doing — with periods off now and then. I also think the magazine will rot from the base up if you never do any more Newsbreak lines. . . .

---

4. Janet Flanner, author of *The New Yorker*'s Letter from Paris column.

I was asking Helen today how she liked having had nine months without winter and in the ensuing conversation she mentioned your fine paragraph about Maine. We both decided it made real American winters seem the best. But Helen also said, "Andy makes an idyll of it, but your feet get cold." If there were no women there wouldn't be any such brief, penetrating comments as that.

Well, keep bundled up,

JIM

►◄►►

Woodbury,
Connecticut
Fall 1938

Dear Andy:

I just had a roast of lamb cooked expertly (not dangerously) by Margaret, our new maid, who looks a strong fifty but is sixty-eight and has seven children and fifteen grandchildren. We found her on a dirt road near Hotchkissville, which is just exactly 1.9 miles from our house. We got back from New York a few hours ago, worn and a little depressed, the way I have never been otherwise than, in getting back from New York. I can't take it calmly or slowly or happily down yonder. . . . You find yourself drinking. This is a practice I no longer care very much about but fall into, the way a man whittles or eats salted almonds or reads *Life*.

It is nice to be back under the two-hundred-year-old maples and the apple trees. Cows from up the road get into the yard when I leave the gate open and their owner comes for them around one A.M. on a motorcycle. One morning (he having said the hell with it) I heard a cow eating apples under my bedroom window. It was seven o'clock. After she had eaten twenty-seven, by actual count, I got up and chased her home in my nightgown. I figured she must have eaten a couple of hundred during the night; she is up and around, though, giving cider and applejack, I suppose.

I sold *The New Yorker* an Onward and Upward on which I spent a week of days and nights: a report on *Punch* for 1889–91, 1879–81, and 1863–65. The house here holds all the bound volumes from the first one (1841) to 1891. I found myself having to use fourteen different source books before I was finished, checking up on Phil May and du Maurier and when *Alice in Wonderland* was first published, etc. (It was published in 1865.) The library here is wonderful and has every history, anthology, book of quotations, etc., you ever heard of and some fifty nobody ever heard of. I could find everything I had to look up. It was interesting to read that du Maurier, who drew a dozen pictures a week for *Punch* for twenty years or more, was "a satirist of modern fashionable life" and then to turn to that quaint, embarrassingly bad, for the most part, satire. I don't know whether Cruikshank, who illustrated Dickens, ever drew for *Punch* or not, but I think not; anyway, in reading a sketch on him I learned that in his old age he claimed to have written *Oliver Twist.* My mother's Uncle Milt claimed in his old age that he had written "Dixie." So it goes. God knows what you and I will lay claim to in another thirty-five years. I somehow hope I won't get the idea that I am Donald Culross Peattie.[1]

My bottom doctor, Robin Hood, told me he had had a man in his office who was "almost exsanguinated." My favorite expression now for bleeding to death. Fellow had just let his rectum go for twenty years, taking a little iron and liver compound from time to time. Scared Ross into going back to Robin, I think. Ross bleeds. Asses to ashes, I said to him, dust to dust. . . . My dentist says I will have my teeth for "quite a while." My ophthalmologist says I won't need reading glasses for "a time." My rectologist says, well —

Margaret, our cook, . . . says one of her sons works into the incinerating plant where they burn the refuge; has had the job since the Armitage. I'm going to have to combine her with another lady of the vicinity who pointed out a flock of fletchers on her lawn and who also told me of a young man who had passed his civil service eliminations. As far as real estate values goes, she says there is a great disparagement. You begin to feel insane after an hour or so of this. Margaret lost only one child, "a beautiful girl of twenty-four" — Margaret is very black and so is one living beautiful girl of hers we saw. I asked what had carried the other girl off and Margaret said, "Tuberculosis. She got it from her teeth. Went all through her symptom." I'm hedged about by misnamed terrors. Much worse than old familiar terrors you can put your finger on. . . .

I keep reading that France has become a third-rate power (*The Nation* says so, too). Just which are the second-rate ones? Denmark? Holland? Or is Britain second-rate and only Germany first? France third, and Denmark and Holland fourth?

We all loved both your pieces in *Harper's.* . . . Helen is very fond

1. The lyrical nature writer.

of the hens who can sit around singing and whoring. *The Sat. Review* is right when it says you are among the great living essayists. . . . I am glad you are getting out a book of casuals. I have already been through "The Fox" twice. It is swell. . . .

Ross undertook to edit a sentence of mine, which needed editing because I had mentioned two different Washingtons without realizing it. It read, originally:

"Montana, the Dakotas, and Washington were admitted to the Union and Washington breathed more easily when Sitting Bull was shot dead."

Ross tried: "Montana, the Dakotas, and the State of Washington were admitted to the Union and Washington, D.C., breathed more easily," etc.

I told him it would have to be: "Montana, the Dakotas, and the *territory* of Washington," etc.

Finally, I showed him how to change the second Washington to "the government," and everything was all right, but it was fun when we got to the point of parentheses explaining that a state is a territory until *after* it is admitted, etc. I said you can't "admit a guest" to your house if he just happens to drop by, because he isn't a guest until he is in the house. The question of whether he was a guest before he was admitted if he had received an invitation came up, ending in a sentence like this.

We still hope you will be able to come down for Thanksgiving. (We feel very badly about your only having one turkey, worth a paltry half grand.) I'll send you some pix of the old farmhouse we live in. It's not a mansion, just a nice old house, full of conveniences, years, and bathrooms. Joy may not come out of the walls but a great comfort does. Margaret turns out to be one of the great pastry- and general cooks of the state; used to cook for Old Hundred, the fashionable inn down Southbury way.

Love to you and Katharine from us both — and to Joe.[2]

JIM

2. The Whites' son Joel, born in 1930.

Thurber and Elliott Nugent, a playwright and old friend from Ohio State, finished writing The Male Animal *and the play had a brief trial run on the California coast in the summer of 1939 with Nugent playing the lead. There were many revisions, after which they cornered Herman Shumlin, the Broadway producer, and Nugent read the play aloud.*

◄◄►►

New York City
November 1939

Dear Andy and Katharine:

. . . There is good news. Elliott and I have spent ten days rewriting the play and last night read it — Elliott did — to Herman Shumlin. Took three hours. He had never had a play read to him before, but since Elliott had acted in it and it had been produced, he wanted to hear it. Warned us he would just listen and then take the script home to go over it by himself. But at the end of the reading and a short discussion of changes he wanted made, he said he would do the play. This is pretty near a record, I think. Selling a play in three hours to the producer who has the biggest record for success in town and who can have his pick of the play crop. He gave us our first advance royalty check today. . . .

We both liked Shumlin a lot. He is a quiet, solid gentleman, very polite but straightforward, not a bully. . . . I was prepared, if he didn't like certain parts, to say no, but he liked the important things and objected only to the last part of the third act, which I hadn't liked anyway. It got trite and hurried, and seemed heavily plotted, and fixed things up too patly. I can do it and get it right. He counts on opening the play here New Year's week. Even that is rushing it a lot. We'd have to play Xmas week in a tryout city. I am confident that we have a swell play now, and that it will be a big hit. I think as big as *Life with Father.* I saw that one night, and my own play twelve times. It was wildly received in San Diego, Santa Barbara and Los Angeles, even when it was full of dull spots and bad writing and some gags that creep in when your back is turned. The theatre would drive you nuts in a week, White. I did some fancy screaming myself. Shumlin wants Elliott for the lead since we can't get Leslie Howard or [Burgess] Meredith. Elliott did it very well and will do it better now that his part has lost an uncertainty which was in it. We may get Peggy Conklin for the girl. Shumlin even thought of Jean Arthur, who would be ideal, but I don't think she would do it.

Life with Father is much better, I think, than when you saw it. Plays have a way of improving 75 percent after they leave their Skowhegans. . . . God knows you get all kinds of viewpoints. Everybody wants to change this or that or put in business or suggest lines. When I got out there (California) the play had lines in it and business suggested by secretaries, cousins, mothers, batboys, doormen, and little old women in shawls.

You got to come down for the opening. . . .

I go on "Information Please" next Tuesday night.

This is James Thurber saying — goooood nite!

JAMES THURBER
the Boy Artist

to

HERMAN
AND
DOROTHY MILLER

*H*erman and Dorothy Miller were Thurber's dearest friends in his home-town, Columbus, Ohio. Herman was for many years a member of the English faculty at Ohio State University, and their friendship ripened in 1922 when they acted together in an amateur production of short plays, one by Thurber. It was one of Thurber's unfulfilled dreams that they would someday collaborate in the successful dramatization of Henry James's novel The Ambassadors.

In 1940 Miller wrote an affectionate sketch of his friend, from which these details are quoted:

James Thurber grew up in Columbus, Ohio, on a street called Gay. He himself would not have seemed too gay; he probably played very seriously. For instance, when they once played William Tell, he stood up solemnly with an apple on his head and allowed another boy to shoot an arrow at it. The arrow missed the apple, but it did not miss Jim's eye. Since then James Thurber has looked at the world through only one eye.

In time he came to Ohio State University where he encountered the President, Dr. William Oxley Thompson, a distinguished educator and a very understanding man. Thurber wanted to edit the college humorous magazine, but he was ineligible because he had accumulated more demerits in military training than anybody ever had before.

"Mr. Thurber," asked the President sharply, "since your record shows that you cannot meet even our ordinary requirements, why should you be allowed to take on the additional work of editing a magazine?"

"Because," Thurber answered solemnly, "when I leave the university, I expect to be the editor of some national magazine."

Dr. Thompson's face relaxed into a smile. "Well, Jim, that's just about as good a reason as I can think of. I'll cancel those demerits." He did. Jim became editor of the Sun Dial, writing most of the copy and filling in the blank spaces with scrawly drawings that were, one day long after, to be famous.

At the university he also met one or two of those rare teachers able to stimulate one to find and love the best in books. Most notable among these was Joseph Russell Taylor who taught him, among other things, to appreciate the novels of Henry James.

One evening in March 1927, when he was a reporter on the New York Evening Post, I sat with him in his little apartment. He was unusually happy that night, for a humorist, but not a little worried. He had just been offered two jobs; and he is not a man to make any kind of decision easily. But that night he finally chose the position offered by Editor Harold Ross of The New Yorker.

One of his major duties was to think up some simple system to eliminate confusion in the editorial procedure. As you may have guessed, he would hardly be the best man for this. As he sat at his desk thinking, he would cover reams of paper with most bewildering line drawings. Although these were only outlines, they were sharp, clean-cut, and startlingly suggestive of action. It was the look of the people that was bewildering, the men seeming

"Stop me!"

to be made of putty and the women of flame. And there were animals too, especially dogs. Dogs by the hundreds. The desk and floor were covered with them. These fell under the keen eye of E. B. White. He liked them and submitted some of them to the art staff of the magazine. Ultimately they were accepted. Thurber drawings came to be exhibited in art galleries both here and abroad. It might interest you to know that one widely exhibited drawing still bears the imprint of a rubber heel; it was among those that lay on the floor of The New Yorker office.

In June 1935 Thurber and his second wife, Helen Wismer, were married. After their honeymoon they spent the latter part of the summer in a cottage belonging to Helen's parents in Colebrook, Connecticut, and there she experienced the ordeal of driving with Jim in the dark.

◄◆►

Colebrook,
Connecticut
August 1935

Dear Herman and Dorothy:

. . . Helen and I have just returned from dinner at the Elm Tree Inn in Farmington, some twenty miles from our little cot. It was such a trip as few have survived. I lost eight pounds. . . . I can't see at night and this upset all the motorists in the state tonight, for I am blinded by headlights in addition to not being able to see, anyway. It took us two hours to come back, weaving and stumbling, stopping now and then, stopping always for every car that approached, stopping other times just to rest and bow my head on my arms and ask God to witness that this should not be.

Farmington's Inn was built in 1638 and is reputed to be the oldest inn in these United States. I tonight am the oldest man. . . . A peril of the night road is that flecks of dust and streaks of bug blood on the windshield look to me often like old admirals in uniform, or crippled apple women, or the front end of barges, and I whirl out of their way, thus going into ditches and fields and up on front lawns, endangering the life of authentic admirals and apple women who may be out on the roads for a breath of air before retiring. . . .

Five or six years ago, when I was visiting my former wife at Silvermine, she had left the car for me at South Norwalk and I was to drive to her house in it, some five miles away. Dinner was to be ready for me twenty minutes after I got into the car, but night fell swiftly and there I was again. Although I had been driven over that road 75 or 100 times, I had not driven it myself, and I got off onto a long steep narrow road which seemed to be paved with old type-writers. After a half hour of climbing, during which I passed only two farm boys with lanterns, the road petered out in a high woods. From far away came the mournful woof of a farm hound. That was all. There I was, surrounded by soughing trees, where no car had ever been before. I don't know how I got out. I backed up for miles, jerking on the hand brake every time we seemed to be falling. I was two hours late for dinner.

In every other way I am fine. I am very happy, when not driving at night. And my wife is very happy too, when not being driven by me at night. We are an ideal couple and have not had a harsh word in the seven weeks of our married life. Even when I grope along, honking and weaving and stopping and being honked at by long lines of cars behind me, she is patient and gentle and kind. Of course, she knows that in the daytime, I am a fearless and skilled driver, who can hold his own with anyone. It is only after nightfall that this change comes upon me. I have a curious desire to cry while driving at night, but so far have conquered that, save for a slight consistent whimpering that I keep up — a sound which, I am sure, is not calculated to put Helen at her ease.

Looking back on my hazardous adventures of this evening I can see that whereas I was anguished and sick at heart, Helen must have felt even worse, for there were moments when, with several cars coming toward me, and two or three honking behind me, and a curved road ahead, I would take my foot off of everything and wail, "Where the hell am I?" That, I suppose, would strike a fear to a woman's heart equaled by almost nothing else. We have decided that I will not drive any more at night. Helen can drive but she has been out of practice for some years. However, she is going to get back into it again. She can see. She doesn't care to read, in the *Winsted Evening Citizen*, some such story as this:

Police are striving to unravel the tangle of seven cars and a truck which suddenly took place last night at 9 o'clock where Route 44 is crossed by Harmer's Lane and a wood road leading to the old Beckert estate. Although nobody seems to know exactly what happened, the automobile that the accident seemed to center about was a 1932 Ford V-8 operated by one James Thurberg. Thurberg, who was coming into Winsted at 8 miles an hour, mistook the lights of Harry Freeman's hot-dog stand, at the corner of Harmer's Lane and Route 44, for the headlight of a train. As he told the story later: he swerved out to avoid the oncoming hot-dog stand only to see an aged admiral in full dress uniform riding toward him, out of the old wood road, on a tricycle, which had no headlights. In trying to go in between the hot-dog stand and the tricycle, Thurberg somehow or other managed to get his car crosswise of all three roads, resulting in the cracking up of six other cars and the truck. Police have so far found no trace of the aged admiral and his tricycle. The hot-dog stand came to a stop fifteen feet from Thurberg's car.

We got the Ford on Martha's Vineyard, where we spent July. Now we are at Colebrook, Conn., or rather three miles out of it at the summer cottage of Helen's parents. It is a delightful place and why don't you motor here and visit us for a while? . . . You'll like my wife and she already knows she will like you. She is as calm as ice when I am driving at night, or as cold anyway.

Love,

JIM

◄◄►►

Litchfield,
Connecticut
October 1936

Dear Herman and Dorothy:

. . . Look, we're coming to Columbus for Thanksgiving and want to set aside a rip-roaring night or two with youse. We'll be there from Wednesday before Thksgvg until about a week after. Let me know what's best for you. . . .

Why does Henry James have to be dead? Goddam it, people are always crocking off at the wrong moment. Speaking of Henry, I went down to my first wife's home and got the set of H.J. she once gave me for Christmas and I have been reading some of the seventeen volumes I never had read. . . . I had never, God bless my soul, read *The Spoils of Poynton.* What a nicely glowing point of honor he put upon two people for giving up Love for a principle! It seems so faraway in this day when we give up principles for Love — and somehow the Love they gave up seems, God help us all, rather more worth the having, and the principles not so much. He would have been most unhappy now, I'm sure, in an age when the male sometimes doesn't even take off his hat or the woman her overcoat. (In bed, of course, I me , There's an essay in it, my friends. Apropos of the present fun that pops up out of his faint far adorations, look at this from *The American:*

> She came in at last, after so long an interval that he wondered if she had been hesitating. She smiled at him, as usual, without constraint, and her great mild eyes, while she held out her hand, seemed to shine at him perhaps straighter than before. She then remarkably observed, without a tremor in her voice, that she was glad to see him and that she hoped he was well.

Their candles burnt at one end and they will last the night.

We went to Boston last week and saw all nine Noel Coward plays and I wrote about them, and drew pictures, for *Stage.* We had dinner with Coward, just the three of us, a lovely time, a swell fellow. I loved his plays, too, and he dashed them off all this summer.

And, I just finished for *The Saturday Review* a piece on a book they sent me called *Be Glad You're Neurotic*. I am doing — have done four chapters already and the *NYer* has taken them, an inspirational book of my own, to be called *Let Your Mind Alone!* I want you to see it and will probably bring galley proofs. Beware of the Thurbers bearing galley proofs. I've had to read the most incredible crap — dozens of books like *How to Worry Successfully* — but filled with such a walking into my spider trap as you wouldn't believe. Or maybe you would.

We have taken the most charming house in Litchfield, the loveliest of towns. I would God you two were the tender apple blossom and could be shipped here in a sachet bag. We have three bedrooms, three baths, three everything. Acres of elms and maples. Across the road is the house in which Henry Ward and Harriet Beecher were born. Down the road is the birthplace of Ethan Allen. Around the corner is a house built by a Colonel Tallmadge of Washington's staff. In it the colonel's great grand-daughter lives, now ninety-six. It is all the most beautiful place! You'd love it. Write me, write us. Box 611, Litchfield, Connecticut, or just Litchfield. I've joined the men's forum and am known.

Love to you both, and we'll be seeing you.

JIM & HELEN

►◄►►

West Cornwall,
Connecticut
January 1937

Dear Herman and Dorothy:

Why don't you answer my drawings? Here I keep sending you lovely pictures of myself and Vachel Lindsay that wonderful night at Dr. Berg's and no answer. Meanwhile, Helen and I have been going around with Noel Coward. . . . He lets people talk and is very attentive.

I am studying Colonial architecture now, and also music. The broken-pedimented round-headed sidelighted doorway, and the contrabassoon. My dream is to sit in such a doorway, playing the contrabassoon. God, what an instrument. Noel is studying German. I sent him a line from the chorale finale of Beethoven's Fifth (or is it Ninth?): *So pocht das Schicksal an der Pforte*, and the translation "Thus Fate knocks at the door." We must all study German. When

Fate knocks in German, by God you hear it. It might be Mort Bod-fish[1] falling backstage. Certainly it is no pansy Fuller Brush man tapping. *So pocht das Schicksal an der Pforte.* Have I got that right?

I am having a show of my drawings in London S.W.1, England, during the coronation.[2] Also one in Hollywood next month and in San Francisco in March. I have on hand enough drawings left to have several more. Do you want a show of mine? I have done, or am about to do, a picture called "Dr. Snook and Psyche" after the famous Cupid and Psyche painting.

The New Yorker gave me 100 shares of stock to keep me quiet, or shut my mouth, or something, and Helen and I may sell some of it and go to Europe in May for my show — and for other things; maybe not for the show. I went to one show of mine and that may be enough. . . .

Love from Helen, and me,

J*IM*

1. A classmate at Ohio State who once fell down while performing in a play that Thurber had written.
2. George VI was crowned May 12, 1937.

►◄►►

West Cornwall,
Connecticut
1939

Dear Herman and Dorothy:

We never did thank you for the flowers. My mother appreciated them a great deal. It was nice seeing Herman if only for such a little while, and we are still sad about missing Dorothy. Sometime soon we will have a long and quiet time together, with just ice water or milk so that Herman's blood pressure and my volubility will not go up.

My mother says everybody will be bad off till 1940 and then there will be a good year till 1941 when the war comes, as prophesied by Evangeline Adams.

We must make the most of 1940, my dears. Let's start planning it soon, that one year of brightness.

One of these days I'll write you a letter.

All our love,

JIM

"*Sometimes the news from Washington forces me to the conclusion that your mother and your brother Ed are in charge.*"

After the New York opening of The Male Animal:

◄◄▻►

Les Revenants
Bermuda
March 19, 1940

Dear Herman and Dorothy:

I don't know what you can think of us for not replying to what, believe it or not, comes to three separate communications from you: the telegram about the play, the letter before Christmas, and the letter about the two magazine boys. . . .

What happened was that Helen and I both went to pieces physically at once, nervously, and mentally, too, I guess. I have been until just a few days ago a shadow of my former self, a shell, a relic, and an old pooh-pooh. From about the time of your first letter I began to lose grip, what with rewriting the damn play, staying up too late arguing and fussing, smoking too early in the day and too often, and drinking too much. The tryouts in Princeton and Baltimore took a lot out of us and the New York opening more. We should have ducked right then but we tarried and had to submit to interviews and God knows what else every day for weeks; I also had to do most of the publicity drawings and stories. We didn't get a moment of rest or quiet and nobody heard from us at all. Every day I counted on being able to write, but I just wasn't. I figure we both lost about ten pounds — I was described in interviews as "emaciated," "painfully thin," "peaked," "moribund" and "washed up." Helen's collapse was fast and bad: she was taken to the hospital, where she stayed two weeks with a blood count so low they were scared to death of leucoemia or leuchoemia or whatever it is. She only had six red corpuscles left and four white ones. They jabbed her full of liver extract and she gradually came up out of the vale. Meanwhile I was down in bed in the hotel, running a fever, seeing mice with boxing gloves on, and the like.

They finally bundled us on a ship for Bermuda and we are just now beginning to get some color in the cheeks and some flesh on the bones. And the strength and the spirit to be able to write a letter. We have rented through May a lovely old house down here on a turquoise bay with birds and flowers all about. The weather has just got fine and the light bright enough for me to see by — for my eyes took a header with the rest of me and for a while all I could see was the larger neon signs and 45-point type. That also kept me from quill and typewriter.

Enough of us. Now about you. We were surprised and also delighted to know that you have given up that teaching job because we knew it was getting you down and because we always wanted you to get to writing. It would have to come when I was in no state to answer your letter with words of cheer. However, better late than never.

I want to know what you are doing and what you have in mind. I worry about you being too sensitive ever to show your things to editors or publishers, or me. I don't want you to get discouraged if something comes back, either. You can write as well as anyone there is. So let us know what you are doing.

As for an agent: I am going up to New York April 1 to bring my mother and daughter together for the first time in six years, or since Rosemary was two, and I will check with the right people and find out who is the best person for you and let you know, if you already haven't done something about it. . . .

The only ideas I have had down here haven't been much. I'm going to do a book of animal drawings for young and old, with text describing them: the bandicoot, the platypus, the coatimundi, Bosman's potto, the aardvark, and half a hundred others. The kind of easy and soothing idea that a broken-down playwright gets. The only book I've read has been *Bernadette of Lourdes,* the amazing and well-written story of the little girl who saw the visions, done by a woman psychologist with no monkey business or shenanigans. It struck me there was a play in that. I wish you would read it.

Our play got good notices and happened to click fast — it's like tossing a coin, I guess.

. . . One reason I had wanted to write you was to tell you that my book called *Fables for Our Time and Famous Poems Illustrated,* which was to have come out last fall but was put by until spring in favor of *The Last Flower,* has been dedicated as follows: "For Herman and Dorothy." That dedication page was set up months ago. You'll get the first copy when it comes off the presses.

With love and kisses and all best wishes, as ever and always,

JIM & HELEN

If you need any money for cheese and crackers until the checks begin coming in, there is no one you know who would more happily, or could more easily, thanks to Broadway, send it. *Don't forget that.*

JIM

Recuperating after a nearly fatal burst appendix:

◄◄►►

> The Homestead
> Hot Springs,
> Virginia
> December 9, 1944

Dearest Herman and Dorothy:

I had a great surgeon, an excellent hospital, and a little help from God & Mother Nature; my appendix was behind my CECUM, and this helped to localize the peritonitis.

Since the Lord wouldn't let me go blind, either, I figure he has something in mind for me to do.

Perhaps it is the noble work of prodding that lazy-minded Herman into writing.

Yes, that is it. I feel it. I shall therefore keep after you. At fifty — yesterday — I feel I have just begun to write. These are the best years. I spit on the grave of my awful forties.

My wound still drains after three weeks, but I'm okay and we go back tomorrow to 410 East 57th Street, Apt. 8D. I wish you would visit us when I get back on my feet. . . .

You will see pieces soon by Peter De Vries, whom I brought on from Chicago, where he was editor of *Poetry* magazine at $25 a week. Thurber, they say, is always right about talent. Get going.

My new fantasy, or whatever, which runs to fifteen thousand words, is called *The White Deer* and is a new version of the old fairy tale of the deer which, chased by a king and his three sons, is transformed into a princess. Suppose, I said, that it was a real deer which had saved a wizard's life and was given the power of assuming the form of a princess? Most fun I have ever had. I even go in for verse now and then, such as,

> *When all is dark within the house,*
> *Who knows the monster from the mouse?*

The Getzloes[1] wired me:

> *You would get well quicker*
> *If you had voted for Dewey and Bricker.*

I replied:

> *The world would be a whole lot sicker,*
> *If I had voted for Dewey and Bricker.*

Let's keep our correspondence going. It's been my fault.

> *Merry Christmas and Love from*
> JIM & HELEN

and thanks for a fine letter.

1. Lester Getzloe was head of the O.S.U. journalism department.

◄◄►►

New York City
January 22, 1946

Dear Herman and Dorothy:

I am enclosing for your, I hope, fond, I have the vanity to believe, inspection, the third or fourth draft of my pastiche, or whatever it is, on Henry James. I spent four months on it two winters ago, but found on going back to it that it needs trimming and changes, particularly in the last section, in which there are far too many poetic quotations and allusions of the kind our poor dear friend would most surely not have indulged in.

Edmund Wilson was all for shipping it off to *The Atlantic Monthly* but I still want to perform a few minor operations. I think that in the main it stands up, but I would like your feelings in the matter. During the four months I worked on it day and night, I was a nuisance around the house because I was unable to get out of the Jamesian phraseology in talking to Helen, the cook, or our guests.

I am planning an extended letter to you, chiefly concerned with the wonderful time we had at your house, and secondly, with a few thoughts on *The Ambassadors* and whether or not it would stand up in dramatization. I have read it four or five times but not since about 1933, and it will be interesting to set down the scenes and episodes that I remember after so long an absence from the company of our poor, sensitive gentleman and his circle. It is quite possible, of course, that when I make this analysis what will stand out sharply and clearly for both of us is the impossibility, not to say the inadvisability, of attempting to transfer to so harsh a medium the last final distillation of what is, need I say, in its original form, the perfect, God save us all, statement of the precious dilemma.

The title seems to me too slapstick or something,[1] and my two alternatives are: "The Larger View" and "The Sharpest Sense." . . .

Yours always,

JIM

1. "The Beast in the Dingle" was Thurber's title when the piece was finally published in 1948.

►◄►►

The Homestead
Hot Springs,
Virginia
December 4, 1946

Dear Herman:

I feel like one of those charred carbon sticks we used to pick up under street lamps in the days when all technics were clumsy and life was fun. I keep wondering what you feel like. Let me know.

I have not been able to write a God damn thing for eight months (or did I tell you that?). Which, combined with a cold and a gloomy view of man, makes me feel like an empty raspberry basket — frail, stained, and likely to be torn to pieces by a little child. . . .

"You gah dam pussy cats!"

Elliott [Nugent] was here for four days and we were braced in the bar by a drunken gent who knew Tom Meek,[1] and who thought Elliott was me. He asked the name of the O.S.U. boy worth a million, who wrote a play with four characters. This turned out to be Elliott (me). To add to the confusion the man's name was Furber.

He asked Helen and me to lunch (Elliott being gone) and turned up with the Dowager Mrs. Cornelius Vanderbilt, who told me she had a funny mind, and proved it by urging us all to join hands and make the Russians like us. She then related how she had called, all alone, on the Gromykos to tell them about her dear friends, the late Czar and Czarina, and their nice, charming circle. The ten days that shook Mrs. Vanderbilt.

> *Love to you and D. from*
> *H. &* Jim

P.S. from H.T.: Mrs. V. also referred to the Russian Revolution as "that time they shot all my nice friends" and said she refused to speak to the Kaiser after 1914 because "he was so deceitful."

1. Thomas Meek, a fraternity brother of Thurber and Nugent.

bering all our fine days together, the suppers at your home, the party at the Whites in New York, the old chalice in Brooklyn, the time I kept going to the bathroom in the chemistry building, waiting for Minnette,[1] and Herman's magnificent laughter when she rode up in a car and he saw she was going to have to sit on my restless lap all the way to Broad and High. I got more pleasure and satisfaction out of Herman's laughter than anyone else's. It was wonderful when his sides actually began to ache and his eyes to stream. I will always remember it.

When I think of Herman, I think of you both, in a thousand ways. There was no other life for him than with you, and you were his complete happiness. You were wonderful for each other, and there is nobody like you. . . . The last time I saw Herman, he told me he was not afraid, but I hope and pray it was not bad. Please tell us what you can, but don't write until you feel up to it. I know you will bear up somehow, and I know you will find serenity in the perfect memory you have of your years together. Few people have had so much. . . .

We send you our deepest love, Dorothy. We mourn with you, and we will think of you constantly. God bless you.

Always,

Jim

1. Minnette Fritts, a college heartthrob of Thurber's.

HAROLD ROSS

Thurber ceased to work regularly in the New Yorker *office after his second marriage, in 1935, but his letters to Harold Ross show that he was occasionally homesick.*

These ruminations were inspired by Allen Churchill, who was thinking of writing an article about Ross and The New Yorker *and had asked for details.*

⤙⬦⤚

West Cornwall,
Connecticut
August 1947

Dear Ross:

We are famous, I was told, for our shyness and modesty. Thus, I was always surprised when anything was printed as coming from *The New Yorker* boys and girls. Most of such anecdotes are either deliberately made up by columnists or are apocryphal in other ways. Gibbs is presumed to have said, beholding the transplanting of a gigantic elm on a Long Island estate at the cost of $200,000, "Shows what God could do if he had money." This is lovely, but Gibbs tells me he didn't say it. His wonderful crack about Max Eastman's book[1] has not been printed anywhere, or at least I haven't seen it. When, in 1929, I felt constrained to advise you where White really was — at the Statler Hotel in Cleveland — because you were going nuts over his disappearance, Andy was hurt because I had promised him not to tell. You explained to him that it was a matter of loyalty. *"The New Yorker* is a cesspool of loyalties," Andy said. I have given this and other lines of Gibbs and White currency. I was a bit depressed when something of my own, of which I was fond, was never repeated to me by anyone. Some fifteen years ago, a gentleman representing an exclusive and expensive special-editions club came to the office on 45th Street and cor-

---

1. Gibbs's reaction to *The Enjoyment of Laughter:* "It seems to me Eastman has got American humor down and broken its arm."

nered me in the reception room. "We want you to do new illustra-
tions for a special edition of *Alice in Wonderland*. To this I replied,
"I tell you what let's do, let's keep the Tenniel drawings and I'll
rewrite the book." The man bowed and left, realizing he was defeated. I burst into White's office loudly repeating what had been
said, but Andy, engrossed in problems of his own, let it slip from
his mind. I happened to recall this some months ago and told it to
Pete De Vries. He put the whole thing in the rough notes of a play
he hopes to get around to in his sixties.

You once showed me [an Alexander] Woollcott letter in which he
said in effect, "Two months ago I did a couple of extraordinarily
fine things for people in my quiet, anonymous way and it is obvious now that they have not been heard of. I count on you dis-
creetly to tell them around." He then told what they were. I have
clippings from various columns of things I have said and twenty-
seven of these were news to me. I make no effort to collect these
columns but they are sent in. The twenty-eighth is from an old
McIntyre column and, wonder of wonders, it was true. In the old
days, you were constantly having partitions removed and then put
back and then taken down again. I put up a sign near the elevators
reading, "Alterations going on as usual during business." A small
thing, but mine own, and the only item in my skimpy file marked
"true."

I can't remember any damn memo of mine at all, but I have the
distinct impression that almost all of them were written in anger
over real or fancied wrongs, and they have more of a fishwife's note
than anything else. I have always been willing to reveal all because
after twenty-five years of journalism I still hate the uninterviewable
person. He is invariably a smug and cocky stuffed shirt.

My chief doubt and uneasiness about a project like Churchill's is
the tone that may get into it — "My God don't these boys think
they're cute." Anyway, White will give a definite "No" on this and
three will get you five that Gibbs will too.

Keep cool.

THURBER

The feud between Harold Ross and Henry Luce was ignited by an article in Fortune *written by Ralph Ingersoll, former managing editor of* The New Yorker. *In retaliation Wolcott Gibbs cut Luce down to size in a sardonic* New Yorker *profile.*

➤◄◊►

West Cornwall,
Connecticut
September 6, 1947

Dear Mr. Churchill:

I enjoyed talking to you and Mr. Carroll the other afternoon and I realize I didn't let either one of you get a word in. I'm sorry your trip had to coincide with Mr. Nugent's arrival and that I had to immediately go into conference with him since he left the next morning. I will promise to be a better host next time. . . .

Ross's faith in the people around him is clearly shown by the case of the late Harold Winney, his private secretary, who defrauded him over a period of ten years of an amount estimated between twelve and seventeen thousand dollars. Ross had placed the handling of his finances completely in this man's hands. Winney was something of a genius in his ability to appraise the men around Ross. When he carried a request for a thousand-dollar advance to Ik Shuman[1] he knew that Shuman would initial it and would not consider it his business to mention it to Ross. Similarly, when in one week he took three sizable checks to the bank, he simply winked at the official who had to okay them. I believe this wink was reserved for the occasion of the third check that week. It was when Winney tried to withdraw Ross's salary for six months that he was discovered. The business department naturally wondered about this. For several days, however, Ross would pay no attention to their phone calls from upstairs because it naturally occurred to him that the whole thing was one of those monumental mistakes businessmen are capable of, since they are all children.

1. One of a series of managing editors hired by Ross.

Ross's duel with Luce belongs in any account of him. It seems that Luce and his men would give out no facts or figures with which Ross could corroborate Gibbs's famous profile about Luce. Ross decided to get him on the phone. The story is, correctly, that the secretaries of the two men got hold of each other but each of the men insisted that the other be put on the phone first. Luce finally gave in and when Ross's secretary said "Mr. Luce is on the phone," Ross casually lighted a cigarette, took several puffs, sauntered over to the phone and said, "Hi, Luce." It was decided in this talk that the two men should get together personally. Luce insisted that Ross come to his house, but Ross asked Luce to come to his house, Again, Ross won. Luce turned up together with his second, Ralph Ingersoll, and found Ross with his second, St. Clair McKelway.[2] The conference lasted until three in the morning, and it seems that Ingersoll and McKelway several times squared off, but no blows were struck.

Ross was handicapped by the fact that he had never read the *Fortune* piece, hence he several times took McKelway into another room to ask about things that had appeared in it. He has always claimed he never read anything written about him and I now believe this to be true. The exchange of dialogue that night which is best remembered by all of us went as follows:

LUCE: There isn't a single nice thing about me in this whole piece.
ROSS: That's what you get for being a baby tycoon.

The New Yorker and *Time-Fortune* had, through the years, taken socks at each other — in our own case often intramural. After the *Fortune* article appeared,[3] White wrote on page 1 of *The New Yorker:* "The managing editor of *Fortune* gets $50 a week and carfare." In retribution for this, White's next book was pilloried in the book section of *Time*. It was attacked and the review was run first. Later, in reviewing another of White's books, *Time* was not only fair but high in its praise. The battle since then has rather died down.

Some twelve years ago when Ross's mother, since dead, visited him in New York, she was, in the tradition of mothers of her gen-

2. Fact editor and contributor to *The New Yorker*.
3. It reported Ross's salary as $40,000 a year.

eration, shocked by Harold's staying out so late. He set aside one night each week in which he accounted for the fact that he got home at three by explaining that he belonged to a men's embroidery class. His mother was disarmed but Ross was faced with the problem of displaying to her some of his work. This came out when he asked several of his women friends if they could get him a doily that looked as if a man had made it. They all said, "No."

His mother was never persuaded that Harold's position on *The New Yorker* ever amounted to much. "I see everybody else's name but I never see yours." He showed her over the office one day but she made no comment. He asked her at dinner that night, "Well, what do you think of *The New Yorker*, Mama?" She sighed and replied, "Harold, I hope that some day you become connected with *The Saturday Evening Post.*"

The small esteem in which mothers of the generation of Ross's and my own hold *The New Yorker* is due to its small circulation, in part. My own mother once heard that I had bought the magazine. She wrote me, "Now isn't this going to be too much work for you?" Another old lady in Columbus said to her son, "I never read *The New Yorker*, but I take it to help Jim."

In spite of Mrs. White's long association with the magazine, Ross is famous for his old conviction that women do not belong in offices. This has mellowed somewhat, partly due to his discovery during the war that several of them could be as competent as men. He also used to suspect that the association of men and women in an office would lead to sex if something wasn't done about it. His oft-repeated sentence in the old days: "I will keep sex out of the office if it's the last thing I do." He gave up after the marriage of Mrs. Angell and Mr. White and that of Lois Long and Peter Arno. Ross is not a psychologist, but he anticipated Miss Horney's "Overemphasis on Love" by announcing years ago, "Sex is an incident." He was always worried by what he conceived to be the tendency of artists and writers toward overemphasis. "Sex is not a career," he used to say.

He also was not surprised at anything an artist or a writer did. He was constantly upset by my lack of tidiness and the litter in my office. I used to toss things I had bought into my incoming and outgoing baskets. Ross had once gone into my office with a manu-

script. I was gone, but White was there. Ross gaped at my baskets and said, "Two cuffs in his outgoing basket and a pair of socks in his incoming." He went away carrying the manuscript. On another occasion, I had bought a large doll for my two-year-old daughter and I had unwrapped it to show it to White. It was a French doll of exceptional workmanship. I sat it up on my desk for a while preparatory to rewrapping it. Ross said later to Mrs. White, in pure anguish, "Now Thurber is playing with dolls. Do something about it."

Some fifteen years ago Ross worried about the tendency of so many casuals to be "neurotic" or to deal with drinking. "Eighty-five percent of the people I know are sound," he used to say. I think he has since taken another look around.

About three years ago I met, in Chicago, a man who had genuine talent in writing and humor. I knew he was a natural for *The New Yorker* and I had him send me a collection of new things written with *The New Yorker* in mind. When I handed them to Ross he said, "It won't be funny and it won't be well written." His quick sense of what is well written and what is funny put him on the phone that afternoon to ask the man to come East and go to work for him. This is Peter De Vries, who has since done excellent things for us.

Just as Ross can discern that a butler is a banker in disguise, he can put his finger on what is wrong with a casual or a fact piece. He invented the word "casual" because that is precisely what he wanted his fiction to be. He was opposed to the formal short story, in part because it reminded him of the big money paid to *Post* writers and others, and the big publicity. It was to get away from this quality that he had the fiction signed at the end. He once said to Sherwood Anderson — who like many other visiting artists and writers from America and abroad went to see Ross as well as the Metropolitan Museum — "There hasn't been a good short-story writer since O. Henry." Anderson loved it. Probably the last formal short story Ross ever read was O. Henry when he was a boy. In the casual he has succeeded in helping to create something very close to a new form. I need not tell you that at its best it is excellent, but that the challenges are rigid and difficult, and it often does not succeed. However, in the case of Mary McCarthy's "The Weeds," which was ten thousand words long, Ross proved that he is never completely bound by any rules of his own. There have been other instances also. . . .

As I said before, I don't want to be quoted except where it seems necessary to your piece. Please feel free to ask me any questions. Again, it was nice to meet you.

Sincerely yours,

JAMES THURBER

◄◇►

West Cornwall,
Connecticut
November 19, 1946

Dear Harold:

    . . . What has happened to Talk has many facets. First, none of us is as young and gay as he used to be and neither is the world. It was much easier to deal with trivia before Hitler. Second, something happened to the general tone of the department when we made over for Colin Kelly and the first days of the war, and later when we devoted the department to the funeral of President Roosevelt. There are several reasons why I should like to see it get back to, say, a talk with the Missing Persons Bureau about the number of letters and calls which still come in about Judge Crater, and things like that. Not only has humor pretty well gone out but Talk of the Town now finds itself wedged in between highly serious and important world reporting and the Comment page of a man who has become the most distinguished political philosopher of the day. We all read and discuss the heavy subjects but we all spend a great deal of time on the same interesting facts, persons and places that we used to. Anybody, including me, could get up two hundred old-time Talk ideas in a week. The thing is to get away from the portentous tone, or whatever it is, and this could be accomplished by a little relaxation of mind and spirit and does not necessitate a tremendous staff.

    I'll go over it with you when I get back, about December 11th.

Yours,

James Thurber

Though Thurber never finished his play about The New Yorker, *he fiddled with it for years. Ross must have suffered from Thurber's leg-pulling.*

◄◄◊►►

West Cornwall,
Connecticut
August 20, 1948

Dear Hal:

. . . I am halfway through the second act of the play, for which I have set a deadline of October 20. There is no pre-production profit on a play beyond the option money usually paid on presentation of the first act. This amount is $500 and, while Shumlin and Nugent, who will produce the play, would probably pay more, I wouldn't feel happy about a large advance on the most speculative of all projects.

It means that I will have to finish three or four casuals which I have either started or will have to start. It will no doubt benefit the temper of my mind in writing the play, since *The New Yorker* editor, to be played by Nugent, refuses to write any more casuals, in spite of his wife's pleas about the budget, because he wants to do a novel. Well, while writing *The Male Animal* I did a dozen fables, ten drawings, a Fourth of July cover, and the book called *The Last Flower*. I am ten years older but I guess I can do it again.

My hesitancy about doing these casuals amounts practically to a blockage, since from January 10, 1947, until July 15, 1948, I wrote seventeen stories and articles, all but one of them for you. I submit that not even Sally Benson, gifted as she is in fluency, has even come close to this mark.[1] It amounted to seventy-five thousand words in a little over a year. . . .

Enclosed on separate sheets of paper are two Talk anecdotes, neither one about children, colored maids or taxi drivers. There are

1. Benson, who often used the pseudonym Esther Evarts, wrote numerous casuals for *The New Yorker*.

also two captions for Hokinson,[2] one by myself and one by my secretary, Jean Hopkins. You will be delighted by both of them.

My pieces on soap opera[3] are progressing well in spite of the tremendous research I have had to do and am still doing. My letters and literature on the subject run to half a million words. I expect to do four pieces, each about five thousand words long. I am even more interested in it all than I was, and the story is amazing and fascinating. *The New Yorker* can put on a soap opera for $104,000 a year, in case you are interested. . . . The time charges for the full network will be $17,500 a week after discounts. I wanted to do this as a hard job of reporting in my old-time manner, when I was just that man from the newspaper, but I find that I can get in as the comic artist and writer. The reticent Hummerts,[4] who own fifteen soap operas and half a dozen other radio shows, refuse to see reporters, so I plied their press man, a Thurber fan, with a long list of questions. Hummert replied through this man that he and his wife had been delighted by the letter, and he then proceeded to answer most of the questions, some of them fully. He said, however, that his wife had lost the sight of one eye in May and that he himself was practically dying. I can get all I need on these people, I think, but it is by no means a four-part profile on the Hummerts. A widow named Elaine Carrington owns and writes three soap operas and grosses $8,000 a week. An underpaid Chicago schoolteacher, named Irna Phillips, began to bat out five a day fifteen years ago and grosses $200,000 a year.

The first piece will deal with the origins of soap opera, the financial set-up, the Hummerts, the nature of these shows, the incredible runs of some of them (six to fifteen years and still going), a lengthy section about one Bob Andrews, original Hummert writer and creator of most of their shows in the beginning. I figure that in fourteen years this man wrote sixty million words. About eight million of them for the first Hummert serial, "Just Plain Bill." For six years he turned out six a day, seven days a week, or about fifty thousand words a week. In the 1930s he wrote a total of twenty-five different radio shows. A good newspaperman for the *Chicago Daily News,* he wrote me a marvelous, long letter about the early days, etc.

2. Helen Hokinson, one of the favorite staff artists.
3. A five-part series on the radio melodramas, published as "Soapland."
4. Frank and Anne Hummert.

The stories of other writers and other soap operas, and the stories of various actors are also fascinating. A man named Arthur Hughes began to play the title role of "Just Plain Bill" when he was forty-five and at sixty he is still playing it. An actress has been on this show for fourteen years, and my friend James Meighan for thirteen. I want to get the stuff exactly right, one hell of a lot of work. I have interviewed thirty people and I correspond with at least fifteen. I hope to get the whole business finished by November first.

In answer to your letter about Allen Churchill, who wants to use memoranda of Gibbs and White and me, I'm inclined to sympathize with your realization that, after all, we are always opening up other people's desks and files. I suppose we should be good sports about it. I think the whole mass of memoranda would be the making of your memoirs — together, of course, with your own memos, which are invariably amusing and penetrating. We have read a great many to delighted groups of cockeyed people.

Somebody once said whereas every word brought out by the old Round Table group invariably was repeated or printed, nothing ever came out of *The New Yorker*.

There is a character named Walter Bruce in the play who has certain resemblances to yourself, but the fellow comes out as a likable, if tortured, gentleman who triumphs in one of the finest hours of the magazine's history, that imaginary day in June of 1949 when, with the help of certain outsiders, *The New Yorker* defeats one George Lincoln Chadwick (Rep., N.Y.), chairman of a new terror called the American Activities Committee. Only you and Miss Terry could be identified by the first-nighters, not counting Dick Maney[5] and my own mother and brother. There is going to have to be a tremendous amount of signing of releases, since the following persons are mentioned by name in the play: Lobrano, Irvin, Arno, Petty, Dunn, White, Gibbs, Shawn, Maxwell, Geraghty, O'Hara, Pete De Vries, and perhaps one or two others.

I am going to let Lobrano[6] read it for suggestions, advice and the possible elimination of tiny matters of dismay which may elude my critical, but devoted, eye. The play is being done with love and best

5. Richard Maney handled theatrical publicity for Thurber and Nugent's play, *The Male Animal.*
6. Gustave Lobrano, the *New Yorker* fiction editor.

wishes to all, and, as Mike Romanoff[7] once said of the profile on himself, it may save *The New Yorker* when it goes on the rocks. The only office scene is the Art Meeting Room. The sanctity of your own office will be at all times preserved. The action covers only about twenty-four hours and if, in that time, we see the going and coming of three different managing editors, it is not such a distortion of fact as you might think offhand. The second managing editor on his first day in the office throws a kind of fit. It is neither your fault nor mine. It just happens that way. . . .

Yours with love, and in no particular haste,

As ever,

JAMES THURBER

7. The restaurateur who became a social celebrity by passing himself off as the nephew of Czar Nicholas II.

◄◄►►

West Cornwall,
Connecticut
December 27, 1948

Dear Ross:

I keep taking a dimmer view of the project to cut up and rear-range the old drawings. Some future day this operation would ham-per and confuse the historian who is bound to write the definitive study of *The New Yorker* artists under the title *Peter Arno and His Circle,* in which I will be briefly discussed in Chapter 12, "Steinberg and the Others." It would be impossible to tell my work from Geraghty's.[1]

I have been thinking about the idea of cutting up and rearranging old captions instead of old drawings. We could get effects like this: "All right, have it your way — everybody you look at seems to be a rabbit," and "That isn't my first wife up there — you heard a seal bark." This indicates that the wife on the bookcase is the man's present spouse, and this seems sounder since it is unlikely that a man would still be fond enough of his first wife to have her around the house entirely disrobed.

If you cut captions in two, dropped them in a hat, shook them up, and drew them out at random, you would avoid simple para-phrase. In one breath you tell me that we have used eighteen thou-sand captions and that we don't use paraphrases. It is almost im-possible to put new lines under old drawings and make them entirely different from the mood of the characters in the original. Take my drawing of the irate husband saying to his wife at a party, "Will you kindly cease calling me Sweetie-pie in public?" I had thought of "Why do you insist on telling everybody we meet that my middle name is Wolfgang?" This is an effort to keep within the tone and character of the couple. You will see at once the awkward-ness and incongruity of "Good God, woman, look out for that Pack-ard! Do you want to get yourself killed?" Or "Get these seventeen coach dogs out of here and keep them out of here!"

---

1. James M. Geraghty, *New Yorker* art editor.

I have just finished two stories besides "The Notebooks" and Helen is overwhelmed by Christmas work, so she hasn't had time to make her careful entry of an old caption of mine she found in a notebook. It is a beauty and there should be a man saying it to a dumb-looking woman. The caption: "You complicated little mechanism, you!" It could fit a four-year-old drawing now captioned "Where did you get those big brown eyes and that tiny mind?" You must realize that this is not a paraphrase of line but simply a variant of attack, which simply has to be used for a drawing in which the original caption has something of the same flavor. In a word, Ross, it is humanly impossible to avoid variants and this is why you and Geraghty hit on the idea of getting new drawings instead of the old ones. Only commonplace figures of nondescript expression will lend themselves to captions that carry no hint of similarity in mood.

Since I am a writer I am not terribly interested in flogging old drawings or whipping up new captions. I also find that I am a little apathetic to the idea of beginning again with the aid of General Electric. Under the best circumstances it would still be a strain that Dr. Bruce[2] would not heartily approve.

Maybe we can get out a collection of our letters on this subject. Happy New Year!

As ever,

JAMES THURBER

2. Dr. Gordon Bruce, Thurber's eye doctor.

High blood pressure had compelled Fred Allen to cease broadcasting and a tribute was being planned, despite his reluctance.

◄-◇-►

West Cornwall,
Connecticut
March 25, 1949

Dear Ross:

I was going to write Fred Allen and ask him to get out from behind that indecision, and let us know if a couple of amateurs like us are going to have, or have not, his support that night. Young Deutsch, as he likes to be called, told me that they might ask Henry Morgan[1] to accept for Allen, but I am sure that Morgan would regard this as similar to Joe Williams accepting for Joe DiMaggio.

Morgan is not a humorist, because he hates people. He hates his sponsors, his audience, and his friends. He wishes everybody were dead, but not in heaven with the angels. I don't think he has mellowed at all. I think he is clucking to the turkey, while he holds an axe behind his back.

The trouble with these youngsters like Morgan and the late Jack Paar is that the lint of the high-school magazine sticks to the blue serge of their talent. I used to do things for the *East High X-Rays* like the following:

Have you heard about the two ways of getting a thing down, pat and mike?

Question: My mother-in-law walks in her sleep and comes within six inches of falling off a cliff behind our house. What should I do?
Answer: Move the house six inches nearer the cliff.

I don't want Allen to leave the air without doing the story of Stanley and Livingstone with Orson Welles, the way they did *Les Misérables.* Allen plays the lost Livingstone, and as the story opens,

---

1. The eccentric radio comedian.

everybody is talking about him. Orson, playing Stanley, says, "You see, it's your show," to which Allen replies, "But I'm not even in it yet." And Orson says, "That's because you're lost."

We now see Stanley on his errand of mercy discovering Stanley Falls, Stanley River, Stanley Mountain, and coming upon a herd of strange animals never seen before by white men. "What are those creatures?" his gunbearer asks. "Those," says Welles, "are stanleys."

Now the big payoff is, of course, the famous meeting of the doctor and the explorer. Welles says the immortal line, "Dr. Livingstone, I presume," and the orchestra bursts into a bright finale of martial music over which Allen has to shout to get attention. "You don't even let me answer," he says. "You don't even let me say that I *am* Dr. Livingstone." Welles says: "We can't distort history, Fred. History records no answer."

This is just a brief outline, but I've dreamed about it for years, and you can send this letter on to Allen. If I addressed him in care of NBC he wouldn't get it for forty days.

Are we going to dress that night, or is it just cocktails? I have a beautiful new dinner jacket, complete, for once in my life, with trousers.

My deepest respects to both you and Mr. Allen.

As ever,

JAMES THURBER

DR. GORDON BRUCE

Dr. Gordon Bruce, a distinguished ophthalmologist and surgeon, began treating Thurber's deteriorating right eye in the mid-1930s and in the course of time was to perform six operations on it. The transition from patient to a devoted, dependent friend came swiftly when trouble set in during a very sunny sea trip to California via the Panama Canal in 1939. Thurber, then on his way to collaborate with Elliott Nugent on their play The Male Animal, *lost his sight entirely in 1947.*

--◄◆►--

Bel Air, California
June 9, 1939

Dear Dr. Bruce:

I guess you better give me the name of a good man out here who can get me some reading lenses. The old eye is the same as ever for distance but I'll be goddam if I can read — except — and this is funny — under a big umbrella outdoors in a bright sun; under those conditions I see to read even newspaper type exactly as well without my glasses as with my *distance* ones (not reading ones — or anyway, almost the same). If I use my right lens as a magnifying glass and pull it away, I can see as clearly for a fifth of a second as I did in 1896. I can also do a lot of other tricks, but I am getting crosser and snappier and sadder every minute straining and struggling to type and to read and to draw (the latter is the easiest). I'd rather atrophy those muscles in two years than by God go through life like a blindfolded man looking for a black sock on a black carpet. If I use the old distance lenses and only have stronger ones for reading, wouldn't that even up on the atrophy problem? Couldn't I go without glasses when not reading, or something? Life is no good to me at all unless I can read, type, and draw. I would sell out for 13 cents. Seems to me the eye began to dim slightly on the third day at sea — anyway I had been able to read for two days and then it got slightly harder.

Best regards,

JIM THURBER

◄◄►►

Dear Dr. Bruce:

I am enclosing an advertisement torn out of a recent *Punch* explaining how to see in the blackout. I have always made a point of learning things from the lower animals because they seem to me to be smarter than the higher animals a great deal of the time. If it is

The White-faced Rage (left) *and the Blind Rage*

going to be necessary for me to tear someone's liver out, I shall have to make a list of the people I want to begin with. "Visual purple" is something new to me and, since I never could see in the dark, I probably don't have any. However, my turquoise blue would appear to make up for that deficiency. Please save this clipping for me as I may want to want to write something about it for publication.

When it comes to comparison with the lower animals, I have found that I see just about as well as the water buffalo, one of the few animals that can lick a tiger. Up to now, the zoologists have believed that the tiger's stripes form protective coloring for him. As a matter of fact, he is striped so that the water buffalo can see him coming. This is my own contribution to the science of zoology and

none of my colleagues know about it yet. Now don't you go telling
them.

See you Wednesday.

Sincerely,

JAMES THURBER

◄◄►►

New York City
Spring 1941

Dear Gordon:

I think you've got something there. Mencken once said that anybody who could think straight could write well. Most doctors apparently think straight. You remember, I am sure, the old nursery
rhyme:

> *I do not like you, Dr. Fell,*
> *Perhaps because you write so well.*

The old rhyme about writers jumping into their manuscripts and
scratching out all their I's doesn't hold in the case of doctors, however. They mostly write about themselves.

Alva Johnston's pieces on MacFadden[1] in the *Post* revealed that
the old boy recommends pulling the eyelids every day to strengthen
their muscles.

I'm adjusted to the new glasses now. Things seem out of the edge
of the lens, curled up like burning paper, but I have got used to
that, too.

I can make out the pencil point now and Helen says I write a
straighter line, though often writing meaningless words. I thought
I would let you see for yourself. . . .

How does it feel to have the same naval rating as Walter Win-
chell?[2]

Remember to pull your eyelids every day.

Sincerely,

Jim

---

1. Bernarr MacFadden, the health faddist.
2. Dr. Bruce had been commissioned lieutenant commander in the United States Naval
Reserves.

◄◄◆►►

Chilmark
Martha's Vineyard,
Massachusetts
July 5, 1941

Dear Gordon:

That thing which was once an eye (*circa* 1899) is holding its own
very well. There is no pain or discomfort, and no irritation from the
drops. I missed only one, and the next day my nurse said, "You are
behind on your drop," to which I replied, "I would rather be behind on my drop than drop on my behind."

The old eye seems to have got immunity to even the brightest
light, and that big blue spot is much dimmer than it was, so that I
am rarely conscious of it. I wore the new glasses for eleven minutes
and then said the hell with it. The improvement in vision isn't
enough to help much. Do you want me to force myself to wear
them, or is it all right to use the others? I go without any a great
deal of the time.

I keep thinking about you and the Navy, lieutenant commander.
What's the news on that? Why don't you tell them you are too
busy? I don't want to have that operation on a destroyer, if I can
help it. I won't let anyone else do that capsulectomy, and I don't
want to wait until you get back from the wars.[1]

Love to you and the cute nurses,

JIM THURBER

1. In 1942 Gordon Bruce was ordered to active duty as a U.S. Navy physician serving with the
Marines on Guadalcanal.

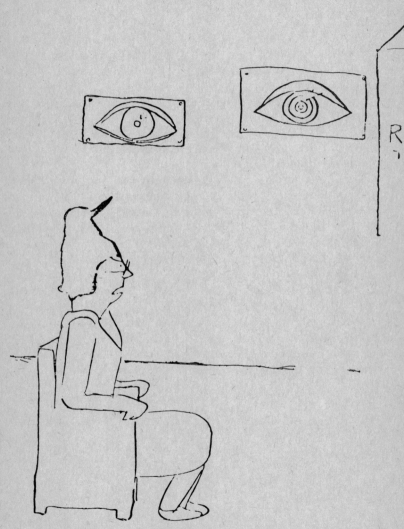

"Certainly I can make it out! It's three sea horses and an h."

◄◄◊►►

FROM DR. GORDON BRUCE

H & S Co. Med. Bu.
2nd Mar. Brigade
% Fleet Post Office
San Francisco,
California
March 7, 1943

Dear Jim:

Yesterday comes a letter from you, dated September 13th? When you wrote it I was in mid-Pacific, and it did a pretty good job of tracing me down across some 7000 miles of assorted elements. It did, however, remind me of the old days when I was an ophthalmologist. Eyes, as I recall them, are little round doohickeys on each side of the nose — or are those dimples? I am free to admit that I was pretty damn sore when I was stuck into the "Malini" (as the natives call the Marines); but I am getting over it. The reason for my rapid adjustment is based on pure conceit — the most an ophthalmologist ever bossed was about 30 beds in a Naval hospital. There are, on the contrary, only 5 Marine Medical Battalions, and I command one of them — the only Reserve Officer, and the only one below the rank of Captain, to do so! At one time, Jim, I had 60 doctors, 1000 men, and two hospitals, under my command; and was responsible for the health of some 12–14 thousand men! Accordingly, I am reconciled to the fact that I am out of Optics for the duration — altho *why* this happened is still unexplained!

The U.S. Marine is a wonder. There are "Guys between him and the seraphim," but I love the dirty, profane, loyal, brutal little reprobate like a brother! He is no ornament for a Victorian parlor, but you can — and should — bet your shirt on him. If we could *only* get him to take prisoners, the little perfectionist! — or sadist, or hedonist, what you will! To me, one of his most attractive features is that he is scared — but there are no external signs permitted to appear, ever!

Dr. Knapp[1] wrote me that you were getting along nicely. I wish

1. Dr. Arnold Knapp, a colleague of Dr. Bruce's who had also treated Thurber's eye.

that I could see you; but as to my former skill, I am afraid that more than a year's absence has about washed it up. Ichabod Bruce, I was knowed as in them days! My friend and boss, General L., is being promoted, and will probably take me along with him. It is strange how much depends upon the toss of a coin — he may go to New River to form a new division, or he may take charge of one of the divisions already formed, which go into very hot action soon. Just the difference between heaven and hell, probably life or death — and I don't know yet which way the coin will fall!

I am asking our Librarian to get that reference for you, the one about the migraine spots.

Give my best to your Helen — and I have seen nobody out here with more guts than her husband!

Sincerely,

GORDON

Dr. Bruce, who returned from the war partially deaf, was decorated with a Silver Star for his service on Guadalcanal, and later with a Gold Star, as recounted in the book A Ribbon and a Star *by John Monk.*

◄◄►►

New York City
January 9, 1946

Dear Gordon:

Helen gave me *A Ribbon and a Star* for Christmas, and the first thing we did was to sit down and search for the passages about you, Brucie my boy. After all your decorations, the only thing left is a suitable monument in bronze, and I keep figuring on the proper site for this memorial. Perhaps it should be halfway between the Medical Center and St. Albans Hospital.

The only reason you did not get your bottom shot off that day, I tell my friends, is because you must have knocked some three seconds off the 220-yard-dash record. I keep the book around to show people.

I never have counted on any further monkeying with what is left of my eye, so you can rest in the tranquil knowledge that I am perfectly satisfied to let well enough alone. It is going to be harder to get an instrument in my eye again than to find you for the next war.

Your suggestion about pooling our resources is a good one, except that my right ear has an idiosyncrasy that might give you trouble every five years. I hope that your ears have somehow turned the corner and that you will eventually be able to hear what people are whispering about you.

I'll be seeing you one of these days.

Yours,

JIM,
THE BLIND HUMORIST

Ha, ha

T.

◄◄◊►►

The Homestead
Hot Springs,
Virginia
March 7, 1946

Dear Gordon:

Thanks for your letter citing me for whatever it is I have that keeps me bouncing back every time I get knocked over. I may be able to get up as fast as a Marine Sergeant-Major but that type seems to stay on his feet longer. Of course, as you indicated in your letter, I am subject to certain attacks from which you and your Marines are immune — it will interest you to know that my chill started this time five minutes after Dr. Canby had identified me with that immortal little prankster.

I can think of no one who would be more amused than you by a certain set of circumstances during my latest fatal illness. After three days of penicillin, I ran one of my atypical and meaningless fevers of 104, and that called in the great Dr. Woodruff, who corroborated my doctor's belief that my two infections had been resolved, so they began looking for a new one. They found nothing but they didn't look into the right place, which was at 55 West 8th Street. Because of the great shortage of nurses, I had to have two male nurses and you should have seen the night man — typical little Village character with a high-pitched voice and a sulky manner who kept stomping out of the room leaving me bolt upright in bed. He smoked cigarettes in the room and appeared to wave a copy of *Life* at an imaginary fly or something. He got annoyed because I asked for toothpaste and said the day man should have attended to that. I got so mad, naturally, that I ran several degrees of temperature. This proves that there are certain areas that even the greatest consultants know nothing about.

Believe it or not, my good man, but this creature's name was Mr. Liberator. We threw him out after two nights when a woman became available.

See you soon if my eye holds out and it seems to be all right.

Jim

◄◄◇►►

West Cornwall,
Connecticut
August 27, 1946

Dear Gordon:

It occurred to me this morning, as it has several times before, that I would like to make arrangements with my attorneys to turn my eye over to the Columbia Medical Center Eye Institute after I have gone to join my fathers. This will not be for quite a few years, I hope.

I have always had a suspicion that I either had two optic nerves or a piece of old pocket mirror somewhere in the back of my eye and if you think an examination of the battered orb would be of any benefit to medical science or mankind, I would be glad to contribute an old useless eye to this end.

You and Dr. Knapp know the condition and history of the eye, but my chances of outliving you both are, of course, considerable, because you work too hard. I would not want anybody monkeying around with the thing who did not know the history of the eye, and that is why you should get around to writing the article on it you once mentioned.

Let me know what you think of this. I am sending a copy of this letter to Alexander Lindey of Greenbaum, Wolff & Ernst since I presume that some kind of codicil to my will would have to be made out.[1]

A psychiatrist acquaintance of mine asked me recently if the brother who shot the arrow had ever married, and when I said he had not the psychiatrist said that this was to be expected. The human being is indeed a complex creature.

As ever,

Jᴉᴍ Tʜᴜʀʙᴇʀ

1. The eye eventually went to the Columbia-Presbyterian Medical Center.

◄◄►►

West Cornwall,
Connecticut
October 28, 1947

Dear Gordon:

When I get back in December from Hot Springs, where your ignorance of the content power of a bottle nipple cost you a pretty penny, I will tell you about the Hummerts. They are the strangest figures in radio and thousands of people would have been afraid to have lunch with them. I kept them sitting until 4:30. (I have been working on a soap-opera series for *The New Yorker* for six months, but it won't appear until March or April.) She seems to have been overcome by terrific fear of her eye condition. Her story of your manning a machine gun is a classic. . . .

The inquisition[1] will probably close in on me soon and I may be led off to the gallows as a dangerous Red. If I am put into protective custody I will send you secret messages. The retinue of persecutors grows very large in Congress. What this country needs is a good detached retinue.

Love to you and Daisy from Helen and me.

As ever,

JIM

P.S. I no longer live in New York but have a house and fifty-five acres in Cornwall.

The eye holds out. See you in December.

---

1. The McCarthy-era investigations.

◄◄►►

West Cornwall,
Connecticut
December 9, 1949

Dear Gordon:

As the result of a piece about me in last Sunday's *Times Magazine* section, I think I am about to be excommunicated. A couple of letters have already asked me if I question the authenticity of the visions of Bernadette, since I seem to compare these with some of my own retinal phenomena. I may have to write a letter to the *Times* explaining that I am a believer in both miracles and retinal images induced by trauma or disease or surgical interference. Years ago you told me about a nun of the middle centuries who confused her retinal disturbances with holy visitation, although she saw only about one-tenth of the holy symbols I see. Mine have included a blue Hoover, golden sparks, melting purple blobs, a skein of spit, a dancing brown spot, snowflakes, saffron and light blue waves, and two eight balls, to say nothing of the corona, which used to hallow street lamps and is now brilliantly discernible when a shaft of light breaks against a crystal bowl or a bright metal edge. This corona, usually triple, is like a chrysanthemum composed of thousands of radiating petals, each ten times as slender as a needle and each containing in order the colors of the prism. Man has devised no spectacle of light in any way similar to this sublime arrangement of color or holy visitation. Now that my eye has involved me with the church, I'll let you out of it completely, because of your exalted position in your profession and in the Navy, and I tell people that my eye doctor was the late Swan Burnett,[1] and that my present man is one John P. Feeney.

It has occurred to me that hundreds of hysterical persons must confuse these phenomena with messages from the beyond, and take their glory to the bishop rather than the eye doctor. This not only obstructs and confuses, but, by mistaking ailment for divine signal, tends to debase the values of human experience.

1. The surgeon who operated on Thurber in 1901 to remove his wounded eye.

I am a believer in miracles, since my own vision is a miracle, but I am opposed to people who can't tell one illusion from another. Maybe I should write a detailed description of everything I have seen, including the battlements which I had for only fifteen seconds one day. I have seen them all and they are pretty wonderful. It is remarkable to me that the surging flow of colors, following an operation, is always made up of restful colors. The central floating spot, in its most agitated state, is a flux of colors very similar to some of the paintings of Braque. The phenomenon of checkered linoleum is similar to the battlements and, like them, has an almost perfect set of geometrical shapes.

. . . Have you ever done a piece on the visions of the human eye? — you can always count on me for local color.

As ever,

JIM

Thurber's last finished drawings appeared in his book The Beast in Me and Other Animals, *published in 1948, although his attempts to draw continued for another decade. Meanwhile sympathetic readers wrote urging him to try lemon juice or other, more exotic drops to relieve his cataract. A kindly Scot even offered to give him his right eye (since Thurber "could make better use of it than I can"), and a South African physician sent advice about special injections.*

◄◄►►

> West Cornwall,
> Connecticut
> December 18, 1950

Dear Dr. Van Der Merwe:

It was kind and thoughtful of you to send me your suggested treatment for eye ailments, and I will discuss it with my eye doctors. I am afraid, however, that my case is much too difficult and special, involving traumatic cataract in an eye greatly injured by sympathetic ophthalmia. There was a recurrence of this after the cataract operation and also glaucoma. It is a museum eye and one of the few in medical history to retain any sight even before the operation.

I am proud to say that I have heard from half a dozen different persons in South Africa in recent years, and to know that my work has reached that far. Thank you again, and all best wishes for a Merry Christmas and a Happy New Year.

> *Cordially yours,*
>
> JAMES THURBER

◄◄◊►►

West Cornwall,
Connecticut
December 28, 1950

Dear Gordon:

. . . You may have heard that Oscar [Wilde] was once sent to a house of prostitution in France, by friends who raised the money at a bar one night, and that afterwards, when he was asked what he thought about it, he said, "It was like cold mutton." One of our present day wits is John McNulty,[1] who had this to say about Lillian Ross's profile of Hemingway: "It was like the Eddie Wakus affair — she loved him so much she shot him." Apparently Miss Ross was bewildered to be told that her piece did Hemingway any damage — and so was Hemingway.

Our best wishes for a Happy New Year. . . .

As always,

JIM

P.S. Edmund Wilson has referred to Maugham as "the gentleman caterer" and Hemingway said of a colleague's sharp ear, "It's the ear of a writer who asks a croupier to give him a list of the expressions he uses."

1. Formerly with *The New Yorker* and a friend of Thurber's since their days as newspapermen in Columbus.

◄◄►►

West Cornwall,
Connecticut
November 16, 1951

Dear Gordon:

Now here is a special problem, which reminds me of an eye doctor you told me about in Pasadena when I was in Hollywood in 1939. I calls this man up and his secretary says, "Dr. Lens won't be able to see you until three months from now." "Tell him," I told her coldly, "that I wouldn't be able to see him then. Going blind, you know."

A friend of mine, Edwin Justus Mayer — whose first play, *The Firebrand,* was more successful than the three he is trying to put on this year, without success so far — has one bad eye and one that he is afraid is "going dead" in sympathy. This has made him nervous, and he came to the right man when he came to me, an expert in nerves and in eye doctors. Your secretary gave him a date pretty far in advance and he has appealed to me to use my magnetism, and my knowledge of your double life, to persuade you to see him as soon as possible.

He has a little money, but very little, so I hope you will go kind of easy, as you do ninety percent of the time, or maybe bill him a few months from now at top rates when he is back in the luck and chips.

I don't know what doctors he's had because I was buzzed when he told me, but I didn't recognize their names. This is a good man and a valuable writer, and we got to save that eye. I'll save something of yours sometime, if you are ever in danger of losing anything.

. . . I will appreciate this very much. Love and kisses,

As always,

JIM

◄◄►►

Stafford Hotel
London, England
June 20, 1955

Dear Gordon:

. . . In spite of the fact that I can see nothing but light now, I am having a wonderful time here in the Duke-Elder[1] country. Also, I keep telling newspaper men how to keep the cat's claw out of the baby's eye, and the baby's finger out of the mother's eye, and perhaps I am preventing a few incidents and lessening the burden of your colleagues. Anyway, I hope so.

Since I have a circus, or museum, eye, it is probably natural that the room should seem brighter when Helen turns out the light at night. I have become so adjusted to blindness now that I seriously doubt the advantage of risking a transfixion. Dr. Knapp once said, "We must treat these eyes with great respect," which means, in my idiom, that I would probably get all the diseases again, with trachoma thrown in, even though I have not even met an Arab woman over here.

Helen's eye is as sound as a dollar,[2] or sounder, and she puts a drop in mine now and then. With Dr. Hartman in Paris and Dr. Duke-Elder in London, I feel much more secure about our three eyes than I would in Bulgaria or Finland. I have not given up the articles about the eye, and you will be glad to know that I managed to send a few helpful hints to the mothers of babies and youngsters on that WOR programme. I always wanted to meet Dr. Duke-Elder, but I know how busy you great men are. I had thought that perhaps an assistant of his might bring me up-to-date on some English statistics about household accidents to children because of cats and dogs and carelessness. You know I am not hipped on this subject, but feel that it is one area of eye troubles in which I might be of considerable benefit to laymen and to doctors. If I could prevent a dozen scratched corneas, or even one, it would be something.

---

1. Sir William Stewart Duke-Elder, one of Great Britain's foremost eye surgeons, whose patients included the Royal Family.
2. She had suffered a detached retina in August 1953.

. . . I must tell you about two young doctor friends of mine, one of them a former beau of my daughter's, who met us at Le Havre and drove us down to Paris. A few nights later, we took them to a nightclub in Paris, which is open from 10 P.M. until dawn. Drinks were $5 apiece, so we had champagne instead, at $14 a bottle. It was excellent champagne and there was a truly fine small French orchestra with a great young trumpeter, with whom we have become fast friends. It wasn't until I began to sing with the band about 5 A.M. that I learned there had been a series of strip-tease acts. When I found this out, the girls had put on their clothes and gone home. I felt that because of my blindness they should have taken at least $4 off the cost of the champagne, or allowed me to touch the girls as they took their things off. But what I want especially to tell you is about the brilliant young surgeon, one of the two Presbyterian boys who were with us. Helen said that when the strip-tease girls first came on, his eyes popped out of his head and he sat transfixed. You see, this was the first time in his life he had ever seen a healthy naked woman upright. He has operated on literally dozens of women, but that is a much different thing, as you know. A doctor's life is not an easy one, for the mystery of women goes out of their lives so early.

> *I am*
> *Forever yours,*
>
> JIM

◄◄◆►►

West Cornwall,
Connecticut
December 7, 1960

Dear Gordon:

As soon as I can get around to it, I want to write an eye patient's report on the care of the human eye,[1] accenting a few of the important things I have learned, since the ignorance of laymen about the human eye and its care is profoundly disturbing to me, as it is to you and your colleagues. I want it to be published in a magazine of large circulation and then reprinted in *The Reader's Digest,* to reach as many people as possible. I get literally dozens of letters from people who have delayed seeing an eye doctor too long, and who trust a member of the family to look at their eye and are invariably told it looks all right. I want to advise them not to use drops, or mumbo jumbo to "cure cataract." I should like to know the name of the condition that superficially resembles cataract and can be cleared up by lemon juice or other citric acid. Thousands of people really believe that cataract can be so treated, and almost everybody, including the so-called intelligent, believe that the whole human eyeball can be transplanted and have no idea of what the cornea is.

I want to tell my readers of the great advances in ophthalmological science since the war. I want to warn people about the danger to the eyes of infants and toddlers from the scratch of a kitten's claw and to suggest that the child always dangle something bright for the cat to strike at instead of the glittering eyeball. I want to tell mothers of infants that they should wear glasses in tending their infants at close range, since George Merriam[2] told me some time ago that as many as two young mothers a week show up at the hospital with their corneas scratched by the infants' nails. I also want to continue my campaign that has the slogan: "Always bring the dog to the baby, never bring the baby to the dog." One of my Scotties, jealous of Rosie, snapped at her eye when she was two, and only a

1. Helen Thurber wrote the article for *The Ladies' Home Journal* after Thurber's death.
2. A colleague of Dr. Bruce's who specialized in treating children with eye problems.

quick reflex movement of her head caused the dog to miss the eye-ball by about an inch.

As ever,

J<small>IM</small>

JOHN O'HARA

The Thurbers sustained a friendship with John O'Hara and his first wife, Belle, over many years, always aware that the novelist's quick temper might turn against them and that silence, for a time, might ensue.

◄◄►►

FROM JOHN O'HARA

Long Island
July 15, 1948

Jamie:

And a happy St. Swithin's to you and yours right back at you!

Fletcher Markle has been trying to get the radio rights for a one-shot of *Samarra*,[1] but as he may have told you, I made the price prohibitive. The girl he had call me told me that she had been authorized to offer two-fifty, and then went as high as five hundred. My price was five thousand, knowing that the show was unsponsored and that no such price could be considered. My chief reason for turning them down was the botch made of *Pal Joey* a year or so ago. It was really dreadful. . . .

Did you ever know that I almost became a producer? I did three polish jobs in four months for Zanuck, during which, of course, I had to have conferences with him and another associate producer. The result was he got old Colonel Jason Joy to take me to lunch and talk business, but Belle would have none of it. I was tempted by the money and security and by the chance to prove that producing was nothing more than shopping at the Farmers Market and charging it to a wealthy, distant employer. I am sure I would have been the worst son of a bitch of all, what with my attitude toward actors (I have two slogans, neither of them original: whenever you don't understand an actor, remember it was an actor that shot Lincoln, and the other, Percy Hammond's, is that the more you do for an actor the worse it hates you); my attitude toward directors (every single one of them thinks he can write, and not a single one of them

1. O'Hara's novel *Appointment in Samarra*.

can); and my attitude toward the economics of the business (no picture ever lost money) and my attitude toward the public (the movie public is the same as the small-town sports in a tent show, who pay a half a buck extra to wait and see "the naked flesh with hair on," and the girl lifts her arm and shows her armpit).

They are not our friends, and we are slobs and snobs when we pretend they are. . . . We are a race apart; apart from our origins, apart from society, producers, publishers, actors, politicians, athletes, procurers, ad men, and lady writers. . . .

The novel proceeds.[2] It will be much longer than I had planned when we dined together, and is now about two-thirds through. I don't work so hard down here, not at writing anyway. In the last months I have been a kind of 1948 David Harum, with a connecting rod instead of a straw in my kisser. The result is I have unloaded my Duesenberg and my Bantam and instead I now have an M-G and a Standard 14. The M-G is the most wonderful car I've ever owned. It seats only two persons and it is so low that I could easily drive under Bob Sherwood.[3] It is supposed to get 40 on the gallon and will go better than 80, which is fast enough for me. The Standard is just as lovely in its own way; it has a lefthand drive, but otherwise it is the car that the vicar comes to tea in. Do you know where I could get a good pair of gaiters? Maybe Halliwell Hobbes[4] has some.

I remain a two-Dubonnet-before-dinner man and there's a good chance that my drinking days are over. I mean real drinking, the kind that a few of us introduced to the United States and that seems to have caught on. I am not trying to be like the aforesaid vicar; I'm afraid. I had a long look at John McClain, who is only from August-to-January older than I am, when he was at the Barrys' over the Fourth, and I hear Gibbs is forgetting to put the cork back again. McClain will be forty-four next month and he looks every day and night of it. That's where you slender boys have it on us pneumatic types. When a fat man gets a headache it isn't time for Pepto-Bismol.

I am pleased that you are working on the play,[5] and, Helen, not

2. Presumably, *A Rage to Live.*
3. Robert E. Sherwood, the very tall playwright.
4. The British actor (he appeared in the 1952 revival of *The Male Animal*).
5. The play about *The New Yorker*.

only do I think "The Chadwick Profile" is a better title than plain "Profile," but I can tell you why. Unfortunately Profile, in 1948, sounds like too many other things. It sounds like a new magazine (to be run by Clifton Fadiman, John Hersey, and a mythical character named Max Lux), it sounds like a B picture directed by an imitator of Alfred Hitchcock, it sounds like a compact, and it sounds like Martha Foley's favorite story of 1950, written by a University of New Mexico senior by the name of Symphorosa Belt, the tender vibrant tale of a Lesbian Navajo. . . .

Now I really must nip off to the beach. Belle sends her love, and Wylie would too if she knew you. And I send mine.

JOHN

I have this writing paper left over from a place I used to work at.[6]

6. The letter was on *New Yorker* stationery; O'Hara was a regular contributor until the late forties.

◄◄►►

FROM JOHN O'HARA

Princeton,
New Jersey
Fall 1949

Dear Thurbs:

By the way what does a thurber do? What is thurbing? "I think I'll go out and thurb the nasturtiums." "Shall we go thurbing this afternoon?" "That goddam thurbing son of a bitch Ross." "Father, the greeve needs a new thurber." All these years, and I never had the philological curiosity to ask a simple question.

Nobody, but nobody, not even Bernard Gimbel, on *The New Yorker* got a book from me. My telephone operator (I have practically a personal one) will bear witness that I tried to get you at West Cornwall the week I got books from the publisher, and the one I am sending you is in point of actual fact one of the first six that were sent me. I called you and left messages at the Algonquin. When finally I did get you (I called the chief operator to congratulate the girl who did the job of tracking you down) I knew, or thought I knew, that your concern for Rosie[1] was the important thing in your life and that it was not a suitable time for sending a 590-page novel. We are glad she is coming along, as glad as we were distressed by her accident. And parenthetically we know what it is to be worried. Wylie[2] has not been out of the house for almost two weeks. A cold led to the return of her asthma, at a time when polio is all over this community. She has had no sign of polio, thank the Lord, but it is when children are for some reason in a weakened condition that polio strikes. It has hit all ages here: a retired Navy captain, fifty-five, whom we know; his fourteen-year-old daughter; the husband of one of Belle's oldest friends; and so on. Half a dozen deaths. Club dances cancelled. The Junior Sports Club, of which Wylie was an enthusiastic member, cancelled for the season. We have our own house now, which is a real break. Dr.

---

1. Rosemary, Thurber's daughter, had suffered a broken pelvis in an automobile accident.
2. The O'Haras' daughter.

Bob Wylie, Belle's brother, won't allow his kids to leave the Wylie grounds. It is like 1916. On the way to the post office I find myself looking with stern disapproval at any group of more than two children. And no man is an island. (Actually I believe every man is an island, but I am only a prose writer.) (Strictly accurately, I believe no man is an island or anything but a man.)

The reviews are almost exactly 50–50. The *Trib* washes away the *Times*, the *Sun* melts the *Telegram*, *Newsweek* does for *Time*, and so on throughout the country as the comments trickle in. The *Times* and the *Daily Worker* were curiously alike, and I mean both the daily and the Sunday *Times*. The lunatic letters have begun: "How could you dedicate such a dirty book to your wife?" The touches: ". . . so if you could lend me $255.00 . . ." The jailbirds — it's a little too early for them and the small-town libraries that have to pay for heat, electricity, pencils, snow shovels, toilet paper, glue, stamps, ink, bindings, furniture polish, extra keys, brooms, and Christmas decorations — but like to get books for free. (They don't from me. From me they don't even get a letter.) And of course the good things, the wonderful things like a lovely letter from old Alfred Harcourt and young Frank Sullivan and other wonderful people, and the iceman, Mr. Kurowski, telling Belle that the pictures of me didn't do me justice, which is quite true so long as I have a tan to cover the scratches of middle age. As to the money, which I care no more about than I do, say, my respiratory apparatus, the book has gone to a print order of 100,000 as of yesterday. It was 50,000 on the print order the day before publication, and they were all gone last week, necessitating two printings of 25,000 each. Well, as Kipling said, the first 100,000 are always the hardest. . . .

I am sending books to Fillmore Hyde, Johann Bull, Herman Mankiewicz, Charlie Brackett, Charles G. Shaw, Scudder Middleton, Ik Shuman, James M. Cain and Ellin Berlin. Also Ralph D. Paladino, Bernard Bergman and Truman Capote. And Miss Tynan. I shall lay one on the grave of Mr. Winney, po' Mr. Winney, Winney the po'.

Now I don't want to keep you from your work. As I understand it you are collaborating with Ralph Ingersoll on a musical based on the life of Morris Markey, editor of the *Chicagoan*, and starring Stella Adler, or *somebody* named Adler. At least that's what I read in Bert Zolatow's column, but of course he never gets anything straight.

All love in the Thurber–O'Hara axis.

O'H

-<>-

West Cornwall,
Connecticut
October 29, 1949

Dear John and Belle:

When my prize collector's item, an inscribed copy of one of the first six books off the presses, arrived in Cornwall, there was a tough struggle for possession which was won by Rosemary Adams Thurber, who is younger and stronger than Helen and me. She had to finish it before she went to Skidmore, which she did by staying up late. She drove the Cadillac halfway to college, showing that there was no trace of psychic trauma from the accident. The final X-rays prove that the injury healed completely, somewhat to the doctors' surprise, since they had felt she might not be capable of normal childbirth. A year ago I sat around in the Algonquin lobby with Charlie MacArthur[1] and Jap Gude,[2] talking about our daughters. Charlie was apprehensive about all kinds of things happening to Mary. At the end I told him nothing would happen to our daughters, and in a year his was dead and mine was nearly killed in a car wreck. Jap's daughter Liz, a lovely girl of sixteen, was the only one to come through the year all right.

Everything kind of closed in on me, and we are going to Hot Springs November first for three weeks, carrying in the overnight bag, where we can get at it, our special copy of *A Rage to Live*. We will finish it in the Blue Ridge Mountains.

We read most of the reviews and the various summaries printed of the source. It is amazing how the 50–50 ratio kept going. This happened to *Madame Bovary* in France, to Shaw's first plays in England, and even to *Alice in Wonderland*, which was not even reviewed in *Punch* the year it came out. Later a Sir Hobart Gill took a crack at it, referring to the text as "those nonsensical legends for the superb Tenniel drawings." The night I was born, December 8, 1894, César Franck's D-minor symphony had its world premiere in Paris. Fifty percent of the audience cheered at the end and the others booed, tore up auditorium seats, and fenced the other side with

---

1. Charles MacArthur, the playwright and screenwriter.
2. John Gude, Thurber's theatrical agent and good friend.

*"She's reading some novel that's breaking her heart, but we don't know
where she hides it."*

walking sticks. The piece is now known as "the keystone of modern
symphonic music." At 245 Parsons Avenue that night, the score
was 4–1 in favor of me. . . .

I am thinking of writing a topical revue, but so far I have only
one blackout. We see Lowell Thomas in the mountains of Tibet. He
falls and bruises his hip, and many voices cry: "A litter! A litter!"
In from the wings left comes Heywood Hale Broun, carrying thirteen collie pups. I have thrown out the scene in which one character
says: "Someone shot Donald Culross Peattie," and another character says: "Ah, another Ruskin bit the dust." I feel that Peattie isn't
well enough known. . . .

Helen and I send you and Belle and Wylie our love and best
wishes, congratulations, and personal regards. It's high time we
saw you. I will be fifty-five in December and on a street in New
York a man recently called to me, "Watch it, Pop."

As ever and always,

JIM

◄◄◆►►

West Cornwall,
Connecticut
January 5, 1950

Dear Cousin John:

The bright moment of the holidays was the phone call from Princeton and our talk with Belle and you, together with the promise you made to meet us in New York on Wednesday the 11th. We will be at the Algonquin and we will phone you from New York Monday to check again. We haven't seen you for what seems like five years and time is running too swiftly now.

In writing my new series,[1] I have dug into family records and find that my mother's great-grandfather, Michael Fisher of Hampshire County, Virginia, married Sarah Petty of Kentucky and had a daughter, Maximilla, who married one Arthur O'Harra, a fellow born in 1801, whose birthplace is not given. There are many misspellings in the Fisher records, and I am sure the extra *r* doesn't belong there. The sketchy family tree refers to "The O'Harra Sketch," giving a page in some book I haven't found yet. There is much internal evidence, in you and me, to establish the definite likelihood that we are cousins, and I have always suspected this.

Hampshire County is now in West Virginia, and my mother recently wrote me, "To think that I have to find out at my age that I don't come from the Richmond aristocracy, but from the trashy part of West Virginia." I dug up the will of her great-great-grandfather, Michael's old man, who was a blacksmith and left "one negro wench named Fan" and "some portable property," probably his anvil. The Fishers had large and sinewy hands and when his will begins "Being weak of body," it probably meant that he could no longer take on his six sons in a horse wrassle.

1. Published in *The New Yorker* as "Photo Album," then in book form as *The Thurber Album* (1952).

You all goin' to be with us Wednesday — heah? Happy New Year from us all.

As ever,

JIM

P.S. Rosie was delighted at the idea of going to the symphony with you and kept saying, "Are you *sure?*"

◄◄►►

West Cornwall,
Connecticut
June 26, 1951

Dear Cousin Jack:

I have owed you one letter since January 8 and a second letter since June 8, and this here is the only letter I've written to anyone except my family since I hit the pier in New York from Bermuda. My brother Robert took a Freudian, or F. Frank Flesh dive off the high board after reading my piece on my father and I have had to quiet him down with common sense, which he won't accept, and about eight letters in praise of the piece, which he does seem to accept. One of these came from Frank Sullivan — a mighty fine boy, with a knowledge of writing. My family kept looking for the laugh all the time, didn't find the ones that were there, and — but this happens to everybody, I guess. Anyway, they liked the piece on my mother, which is in proof, but God knows what Sayre's cover story in *Time*, coming out in the issue of July 9, will do to them, since, once again, a piece about the family fails to mention that my father was President of the United States and left three million dollars when he died, which seems to be my family's estimate of success. . . .

I like short novels, of the size you are now writing, whether it is the size of *Hope of Heaven* or *A Lost Lady* or even *My Mortal Enemy*. This last is as close as any, I suppose, to what Henry James called the "novella," but it is a length that annoys publishers, I hope. I once asked Simon & Schuster what they meant by "full length," explaining that *The 13 Clocks* was not going to run to sixty thousand words. Books of a size like *Appointment in Samarra* or *The Great Gatsby* are good-sized books.

I have yelled myself hoarse at Ross about various phases of the magazine and have given up on the ground that I am too old. Right now the boys and girls are all bothered about Dale Kramer's *Ross and the New Yorker*, to be published this fall. I damn near wrote a piece about that awful [A. J.] Liebling review, even started it, but got overwhelmed by other stuff, since I am working on two books now and want to turn them in soon in order to have time to monkey with the play. This business of lifting short excerpts is lousy, but I was even more annoyed by his attempts at humor, in parentheses, which fell flat, and by his pontifical crap about the Pep West novel[1] being better than *The Last Tycoon.* I couldn't get through the West thing, which seemed to me an underwater view of minor grotesqueries as against Fitzgerald's clear long view of Hollywood as a whole, in which grotesqueries took their proper place. . . .

Love and kisses,

As always,

JIM

1. Nathanael West's *The Day of the Locust.*

In sympathy, after Belle's funeral:

◄◄►►

West Cornwall,
Connecticut
January 15, 1954

Dear John:

There wasn't a chance for a private and personal word, so I've got to put them down on paper. There wasn't a person there who didn't mention how wonderful you were through it all. The one bright touch for me was your daughter and the fact that you have her. They are indispensable and become increasingly more so in a man's life. Everybody said she has Belle's smile and I am glad that smile still goes on in this world. I became very close to Belle during our ordeals of last summer and she did a great deal for me. She always said enough, but never more than that. I see her on a lot of bright corners of recent years, going back to those days in London. My God, that was more than fifteen years ago, but it was just yesterday, too. . . .

Whenever you feel like it, John, write to me. I'll be up here finishing a book and crawling out of the ruins of this month's taxes. Give my love to Wylie and tell her I won't forget to send her something nice next June 14. She shares her birthday with the American flag and I share mine with one of the big holy days of the Catholic year. Love to you both from Helen and me. I wrote Rosie and she would put her love in here, too.

As always,

JIM

P.S. We rode back with your brother Joe, and he told some wonderful stories of the O'Hara home when you were seventeen and eighteen and his idol. He must have been a blessing to have around

in hours of crisis. Our phone number up here is Orleans 2-6557.
We live a mile from a village and have one more digit than the
Columbus, Ohio, phones, and that city is going on 400,000 in pop-
ulation.

◄◆►

West Cornwall,
Connecticut
March 25, 1959

Miss Beverly Gary
New York Post
New York City

Dear Miss Gary:

. . . You can say I said this: John O'Hara, being both Irish and artist, is doubly interesting, twice as complicated and maybe three times as difficult as he would be if he were only one of those volatile beings. He likes to admit he is wrong when he is but he doesn't like to be told it. Being ambivalent, even dichotomous, he would go through the smoke and flame for a friend, and often has, but he has a quick Irish-artist tendency, now and then, to strike friends "off the list," as he calls it. This is sometimes a permanent consignment to limbo, but oftener just a temporary term in Coventry. I have been a friend of O'Hara's for thirty years, off and on, but mostly on. The only tough assignment we ever had occurred about 1945 because of a certain name applied to O'Hara, not by me, but by him. He called himself this ugly name, and I told him he was a liar and he was not that, and this annoyed O'Hara, O'Hara being O'Hara. He can almost always tolerate a major aggression, but takes fire about minor misunderstandings, and thus gained the name of being "Master of the Fancied Slight." I did not apply this to him and do not know who did. He writes ·wonderful letters and I've got quite a few while working on the Ross book,[1] but have apparently been off the list for some months now. I don't know why. I guess a man cannot have an ear and eye and mind as sensitive as O'Hara's without also having feelings that are hypersensitive. He is, of course, one of the major talents of American literature. He brings into a room, or a life, the unique presence that is John O'Hara. If he sometimes seems to exhibit the stormy emotions of a

---

1. Thurber's *The Years with Ross.*

little boy, so do all great artists, for unless they can remember what it was to be a little boy, they are only half complete as artist and as man. Who wants to go through life with only easy friends? Nothing would be duller. That reminds me of Meredith's —

> Would we through our lives love forego,
> quit of scars and tears?
> Ah, but no, no, no.

Sincerely yours,

JAMES THURBER

TO WHOM IT MAY CONCERN

‑◄◇►‑

West Cornwall,
Connecticut
December 26, 1952

Mr. Wainwright Evans
New City
Rockland County, New York

Dear Mr. Evans:

I don't know what made you think that my great friend Nugent is psychic or touched by the unexplainable. This makes you as wrong as a Duke dice girl trying to throw thirteen.[1]

My mother, who is eighty-seven, and I have always taken mental telepathy in our stride and we regard it as far less remarkable than television, the trans-Atlantic cable, or even the telephone. Most of our achievements in this field of mental phenomena have been trivial, such as my saying to my first wife, as our train pulled out of South Norwalk, "Norman Klein just got on this train about three coaches up," and my mother's saying, at an 1898 party, "Sam Pancake will be about to ring the doorbell when I reach the front porch." Norman Klein was on the train all right, for the first time in maybe ten years, since it wasn't his regular road, and Pancake had his finger on the doorbell. The remarkable thing about him was his name and the fact that he was known to be out of town at the time. "Came back suddenly and heard about the party," he said.

Mamma and I have done literally hundreds of things like this, and we used to put on our exhibition of parlor telepathy almost without a miss when she was younger. Everybody thought it was a trick. I would spread twenty-five different objects on the floor and think of one of them, and she would pick it out. We were not visible to each other at the time, nor did we speak.

It used to be nothing for me to say to my brother, as I did one day, ten blocks from the State House in Columbus, Ohio, "Ray Jackson is in the rotunda." He would bet a couple of bucks, being

---

1. An allusion to the Duke University psychokinesis experiments.

too smart to wager a fortune. Well, Jackson was there all right that day, a Columbus photographer then about forty-five, who said to us, "I've never been in this rotunda before and I just decided to come in and see what it's like. I suppose I've gone through the State House grounds two thousand times without thinking of entering the building."

The only valuable piece of communication that I have experienced in this line hit me one morning in 1900 when I was six years old. I was playing about six blocks from home with some kids when I realized that my four-year-old brother was in some kind of danger. I ran all the way home to find that he had set his bed on fire by playing with a buggy whip and dangling the lash in a lighted gas grate. I mention this incident in *The Thurber Album*, leaving out the psychic factor. My mother got him off the bed before the flames reached him. He had been asleep and the heat had given him a sense of danger. At such times he always thought of me because he lisped and talked funny and I was the only one who could understand him. As simple as that.

I got one of Dr. Rhine's[2] books a few years ago, but it's full of charts and diagrams and too damned technical.

My four-year-old brother, Robert, now fifty-six, must have had a wonderful sending set when he was a child. One Sunday my mother jumped to her feet while sitting with her own mother and sister in the sewing room of my grandmother's house, crying, "Robert has been hurt!" It turned out he had been run over by a milk wagon four blocks away at that very moment. He was six years old then. My father entered the house carrying him about five minutes later. He was not badly hurt. I was in the house, but I didn't get that message at all. Even odder, my mother was downstairs at the moment her youngest son was about to burn up and she didn't know it until I dashed into the house and told her.

Makes you stop and think, doesn't it, Evans? Merry Christmas and a Happy New Year.

Sincerely yours,

JAMES THURBER

2. Joseph Banks Rhine, the controversial psychologist who ran the Duke parapsychology laboratory.

◄◄►►

West Cornwall,
Connecticut
September 12, 1956

Mr. Alan Jay Lerner
New York City, New York

Dear Mr. Lerner:
. . . Chaplin's critical sense was erratic and almost unbelievable. I met him only once, in Hollywood, and after he had showed off and talked a lot of rapid and confused social philosophy, he told me I had written one of the two funniest things in the world. Turned out that what he had in mind had been written by E. B. White. Summary: Waitress spills hot soup on male diner, says, "Jesus Christ." I asked him what the other funniest thing in the world was. Gist of his answer: Man is bending over tying his shoelace on a street corner, another man comes along and kicks him in the ass. "What did you kick me in the ass for?" "You were tying your shoelace, weren't you?" Well, there you have it. I was told in London that Chaplin maintains his record for this kind of thing. His favorite remarks in company now are: "The only thing I liked in America was Peter Paul's Mounds" and "All that America can be proud of is a balanced cat diet." He was one of the great comedians, and one of the worst appreciators of comedy outside himself and his own genius. I went further in school than Chaplin and am a more serious character, so my judgments are more dependable.

Thanks for the note and best luck to you and yours.

Cordially,

JAMES THURBER

◄◄►►

West Cornwall,
Connecticut
March 17, 1959

Miss Martha Deane
Radio Station WOR
New York City, New York

Dear Martha Deane:
 I certainly hope to go on your program sometime late in May.[1] I am amazed how you survive all your guests. It seems to me your guests divide into two groups: those experts who know all about a subject, and boast about it, and those authorities who know nothing at all about their subjects and admit it. I should like to go on your program as Dr. Jacob Thurberg, who has spent his life trying to find the cause and cure of motorman's knee, but admits that we are no further along than we were when the streetcar was invented. In spite of motorman's knee, as you may know, thirteen motormen escape every year from Rumania. Unfortunately they seek refuge in countries which have given up streetcars, so the problem is even greater than it was. When I was a little girl of six, my father insisted that I become the world's greatest bassoon player, but to his dismay I became Harry Lorayne.[2] He says he has memory and the ability to teach memory, which is tantamount to saying that he can teach little boys how to be little girls. When he was on your program, he asked you to name five or six states of the union and he would tell you the capital city and population. I made no effort whatsoever to remember the states you asked him, but they are, in order, South Carolina, Missouri, Alaska, Kentucky, and Tennessee. This is memory, and nothing can take its place. Later I became Sir James Thurberville and spent three years in Africa, trying to find a cure for everything in a compound of beetles' feet. Instead of that I turned up, quite accidentally, with a cure for Dorothy Gish. In applying this to the serious condition of Steve Allen, I found that I had no

1. Thurber was often a guest on her talk show.
2. The writer and lecturer on memory training.

such cure. What I had was a solution of the Salvation Army's opposition to marriage outside the clan. It was then that I took up the oboe, and this led, slowly but surely, to my becoming Nelson Rockefeller. I shall be glad to tell about this on your program, and I will let you know when we can get together.

Love and kisses.

As ever,

JIM THURBER

◄◄►►

West Cornwall,
Connecticut
May 2, 1960

Miss Carolyn Wilson
Casey Key
Nokomis, Florida

Dear Carolyn Wilson:

Our mutual friend Libba Thayer has given me your address and reminded me that you and I were great friends of Elmer Davis,[1] so I felt like writing to you. . . .

Elmer Davis was my favorite American of this century, as I have said in private and in print, and I was happy that he lived to read my dedication to him of *Further Fables for Our Time.* He wrote me a brief, painful, but bright note about it, saying that it made him feel like a cross between Abraham Lincoln and Dr. Schweitzer. I know a great many other admirers of Elmer, including Edward P. Morgan, who broadcasts for WABC, and many newspapermen.

I hope that May is as lovely now in Florida as it was when I was there last, way back in 1932. I send you my blessings and best wishes.

JAMES THURBER

1. Elmer Holmes Davis, author and news commentator.

◄◄◊►►

London, England
May 17, 1961

Mr. Milton Greenstein [1]
The New Yorker
New York City, New York

Dear Milt:

I won't be able to finish the Houdini piece until we return to West Cornwall, where I hope my books and pamphlets on Houdini are still to be found. The piece presents two special problems, and I'll be glad to get it off my mind one way or another.

It will be part of a book, for which I have had various tentative titles, the present one being *Yesterday Upon the Stair*. All of the pieces are intensely personal, constituting, in fact, the autobiography of my mental life, you might say. This might easily give the boys at the old plant the leaping gallops, although, come to think of it, McKelway has pretty well written about the same kind of thing. One piece, to be sure, could easily appear in *The New Yorker*, and the others somewhere else, if necessary.

The other problem is kind of amusing, without being hilarious. My story of Houdini properly, and unavoidably, begins with my meeting his widow, a few months after his death in 1926, in, of all places, the office of the warden of Sing Sing, and the fact I cannot leave out or distort is that I was sent up there on assignment by the *New York Evening Post*, which turned out to be a wild goose chase. I don't feel that I can say that I was a prisoner at that time, or an old friend of the warden, or an official of the jailhouse.

As I have said in previous letters, a few of them written when Ross was alive, the Old Boy had an antipathy amounting almost to phobia about stories dealing with newspapermen, because he had been so conscious, all his life, of having been a reporter on some seven papers. . . .

Love as always,

JIM

1. The *New Yorker* attorney who checked copy for libel.

In preparation for an article to be published in one of the Luce maga-
zines, the Thurbers were interviewed by Frances Glennon. There would
be much rewriting before a likeness was achieved.

◄◄◆►►

West Cornwall,
Connecticut
June 24, 1959

Miss Frances Glennon
Time-Life Building
New York City, New York

Dear Frances:

Robert Morsberger, professor of English at Miami University, Ox-
ford, Ohio, has written, and is now rewriting, what he calls a critical study of my work. Today I wrote him asking permission for *Life*
to use, if it wants to, this quote from his Preface: "It is my conten-
tion that Thurber, while one of our funniest writers and illustrators,
is by no means merely a humorist, but an important literary artist
who uses laughter as a civilizing force, necessary to man's sanity
and survival, and whose work deserves serious consideration and
a permanent position in American literature."

Most so-called academic studies of what I write and draw seem
to me to overemphasize the "important" while underestimating the
so-called humorous, alias trivial. I simply say to all this that my
days, nights, and years are an unplanned combination of both elements. If they weren't, I would be all professor or all clown, both of
them good things to be, if they are not mutually exclusive. An evening given over completely to serious discussion is as dull as one
given over entirely to clowning around. After a little of Einstein
there ought to be a little of Cole Porter, after talk about Kierkegaard
and Kafka should come imitations of Ed Wynn and Fields. Humor
is counterbalance. Laughter need not be cut out of anything, since
it improves everything. The power that created the poodle, the platy-

pus, and people has an integrated sense of both comedy and tragedy. Benchley once said, "Only a humorist could take humor apart,
and he has too much humor to do it." Serious definition of a free-
lance writer: One who gets paid per word or per piece. Benchley's
humorous, hence perfect, definition: "One who gets paid per word,
per piece, or perhaps." Which is the more serious, the utterly serious, or the partly humorous? Nobody can divide them soundly.
When we say "psychosomatic" it is both redundant and silly, like
"female wife," because you cannot separate the mind and the
body, or imagination and the central nervous system. The old cliché
"the dignity of man" is proved only in the breach. It is only when
he falls down that we appreciate how straight he can stand. . . .

Cordially yours,

JIM

P.S. I loathe the expression "What makes him tick." It is the American mind, looking for simple and singular solution, that uses the
foolish expression. A person not only ticks, he also chimes and
strikes the hour, falls and breaks and has to be put together again,
and sometimes stops like an electric clock in a thunderstorm. As I
once said about Woman as she grows older, her maidenspring becomes matronsprung. A man once showed a so-called indestructi-
ble watch to Bob Benchley and Dorothy Parker at Tony's.[1] They
whammed it against a table top, then put it on the floor and
stamped on it. The dismayed owner picked it up and put it to his
ear. "It has stopped," he said incredulously. "Maybe you wound it
too tight," said Benchley and Parker together.

Maybe I wound myself too tight. If so, unwind me.

P.P.S. "You are all a lost generation," Gertrude Stein said to Hemingway. We weren't lost. We knew where we were, all right, but
we wouldn't go home. Ours was the generation that stayed up all
night. Indeed, we spent so little time in bed most of us had only
one child (Ross, White, O'Hara, McKelway, Sayre, Markey, Broun,
McNulty, myself, and others). I have stayed up all night with most

---

1. A speakeasy.

of those named, and the first and only time I met Fitzgerald, Thomas Wolfe, and Sinclair Lewis. We changed the sitting room to the pacing room. No wonder so many of my generation have died before the age of sixty-five. The American pace we set was much too fast for life to endure long. I count my generation as beginning in 1889, when Benchley was born, and ending about 1905, when O'Hara and McKelway were born, but most of us saw the light in the nineties. I was born in 1894, same year as Mark Van Doren and, I learned when I met him, J. B. Priestley, who said, "It was a vintage year." Fitzgerald, by the way, had only one child, a daughter. The only night we met, at ten P.M. in Tony's in 1934, we got back to the Algonquin at eight A.M. in a cab. He got out and said, "Goodnight. You don't belong to my generation and you don't have a daughter." I told him I was 1894 to his 1896 and had a daughter. He got back in the cab. "Drive around the park," he told the driver, and we drove around Central Park.

J.T.

◄◄◆►►

West Cornwall,
Connecticut
June 30, 1959

Miss Frances Glennon
Time-Life Building
New York City, New York

Dear Fran:

A few of my own favorite drawings . . . in *Men, Women, and Dogs.*

"What have you done with Dr. Millmoss?"

"What have you done with Dr. Millmoss?"

"It's a naïve domestic Burgundy without any breeding, but I think you'll be amused by its presumption."

"Destinations."

"You said a moment ago that everybody you look at seems to be a rabbit. Now just what do you mean by that, Mrs. Sprague?"

"For heaven's sake, why don't you go outdoors and trace something?" (One of Helen's favorites, too.)

"Well, if I called the wrong number, why did you answer the phone?"

Here we have an aggressive woman, a disturbed woman, a confused woman, and an irritated woman, and an assortment of animals and persons. I'll leave out such too often mentioned ones as The Seal in the Bedroom, The Lady on the Bookcase, and "Touché!"

As ever,

JIM

"All Right, Have It Your Way — You Heard a Seal Bark!"

RONALD
AND
JANE WILLIAMS

In the mid-1930s the Thurbers, who were on vacation in Bermuda, became devoted to Ronald Williams and his young and lovely wife Jane. A native of Wales who had run away to sea at sixteen, Ronald had finally settled in Bermuda to become editor and owner of The Bermudian, *to which Thurber contributed without fee. At the outbreak of war Williams was commissioned in the Royal Navy and felt obliged to sell his magazine to support the family until his return.*

◄◊►

Martha's Vineyard,
Massachusetts
July 14, Bastille Day
(no celebration) 1941

Dear Ronnie and Janey:

. . . The pattern of the old life has certainly changed. We were proud and sad, too, to hear that Ronnie has joined the King's Navy. We know he will become a lieutenant commander, at least. We hope he will make a quick end to all this nonsense, so we can all get together again. It will be nice to have Janey in the States, and we count on seeing you, gal — and Drax, who must be a big boy by now.

The idea of selling *The Bermudian* saddens us terribly. I wish you could arrange somehow to keep one hand on it, so you can get it back when the war is over. Bermuda ought to be more popular than ever after the war. We can't think of Bermuda without the Williamses, and we like to think of Bermuda. We will have to work out something to get us all back there when Ronnie has sunk Hitler without a trace.

. . . I have had five operations on the lone glim since I saw you, and I still can't see. They dragged old Jamie through all the corridors of hell, where I left most of my weight and two thirds of my nerves, but things have quieted down now, and after one more operation in the fall, I should be able to see again, normally.

I send you all my love and all my best wishes, and all hopes of our getting together again before too long. And now, Mrs. Thurber has a message for you.

As ever,

JIM

Darlings:

I should have kept you informed all winter, but things have been so uncheerful that I hated to write. Jamie has honest to God been through the valley of the shadow, and that can have nothing to do with death, I assure you. He had that first, preliminary operation a year ago last June, right after we left you people, and didn't mind it at all. His sight improved enough so that he could see to read and write during the summer, at least until about the middle of September. We came to New York the middle of October, after taking a house in Connecticut for the winter, and he went to the hospital for the big operation, the removal of the cataract, which had developed completely by that time. The doctor had said hopefully two weeks in hospital, two weeks more in town, and then we could leave. Things didn't turn out as planned.

Dr. Bruce told me afterwards it was touch and go for the fifteen minutes of the operation. His eye was so stuck up with old scar tissue from the bad iritis he had had as a kid (when his dumb family waited two weeks to have the ruined eye taken out so that the other got infected) that the doctor thought the whole thing was gone. However, he got the cataract out without taking out *everything*, through sheer skill, but Jamie got iritis, was in the hospital five weeks, at the end of which he developed a bad case of hospital phobia or nerves, and we brought him down to the hotel, where we had day-and-night nurses for some weeks more.

It was the first experience I have ever had with a nervous breakdown, so-called, and it was awfully hard on him. He pulled himself out of it through will power, though. We went up to our rented house for Christmas, for the eye looked better, but up there it took a bad turn and we rushed back, and from then on things were bad. Everything happened to the eye that could. He had another operation in February, another in March, another in April, and another in May. In the meantime, I had closed the house in the country and

rented an apartment on Washington Square in New York, brought
my servants down, and the car, for we had to drive up to the hospital every other day, even when he wasn't in it, for treatments,
and the Medical Center is a five dollars' taxi fare from where we
lived and I am Scotch and that killed me. Each operation was harder
on his nerves (no general anesthetic was allowed, only a local each
time), and he was in pretty bad shape. . . .

Well, we got through that, and the last operation, we hope, was
scheduled for June, as an anniversary present, but as soon as Dr.
Bruce saw that the eye was at last safe, and nothing new or awful
could develop, he advised us to get away for the summer, and save
the final thing for fall. . . . Only Jamie cannot get out alone, has to
be led around, except indoors, where he is very agile. And the
worst is that he cannot read or draw. He writes in longhand on
yellow paper, but cannot see what he writes, and you know his
painstaking method of writing and rewriting. He felt at a great loss,
and still does, but did a casual, a long one, for *The New Yorker* a

short time ago and they are crazy about it. He had to do the first version, and the revision, in his head, then write down the second revision. And it came out swell. He does a weekly column for *PM*, the newspaper, and very well, too, but it is hard to get ideas when you can't read. He is a wonderful man, children, and you would be proud to know him. I cannot think of anyone else, at least among our little group in New York, who could have gone through it and come out sane. But of course his brand of sanity was always different from anyone else's, and that probably helped.

It is lovely up here, more like Bermuda than any place we know, which is why we came. . . .

Our address is Chilmark, Martha's Vineyard, Mass. Janie, please use it soon. Ronnie darling, good-bye and all our love, and come back soon.

HELEN

◄◄►►

West Cornwall,
Connecticut
May 18, 1943

Dear Ronnie:

Four years ago tomorrow, Helen and I got on the S.S. *President Garfield* for California via the Canal (I kept a sharp eye for the S.S. *Guiteau* — the name of the man who shot Garfield). I still had a sharp eye in those days — but it was on this trip that I first had trouble reading. . . .

It was swell to hear from you, but sad to know we missed you on your leave. Let's make a date for next time. It was wonderful seeing you after the long short years, but there wasn't enough of it.

. . . I'm busily at work on a play for the fall — a comedy about *The New Yorker* — and I want you to be ashore to see it. I'm getting two books out this fall, the first book of drawings in ten years,[1] and a book for young and old called *Many Moons,* with lovely color work by Louis Slobodkin (not a Jap or German). Janey got paid for an anecdote I wrote about Mountbatten — I credited it simply to an old English seafaring gentleman.

We were proud to hear of your promotion to No. 1, and glad it gave you a chance to see Janey and the kids. It will be fine if you get ashore for four months. We won't miss seeing you that time.

I'm going to send you a new Maugham anthology of British and American writing — mainly because I'm in it — and the *Best Short Stories of 1943* when it comes out in June (yeh, I'm in that too — pretty good for an aging blind man). . . . I sent two hundred copies of my *Fables*[2] to the RAF during the awful days when they were saving the world, and they got all around. I got an official letter from RAF headquarters in London. My English editions always do well, and for this I am proud. . . .

It's hot enough for one of your great milk punches, and I wish we were all drinking one together — to your health and happiness and quick return — from Helen and

JIM

1. *Men, Women and Dogs.*
2. *Fables for Our Time and Famous Poems Illustrated.*

Thurber came down with pneumonia during a summer visit to Jane Williams, who was spending the war years with her mother and sisters at Long Point, New York. He was still weak when Helen brought him back to New York City, but was able to write his letter of thanks.

◄◄►►

West Cornwall,
Connecticut
September 21, 1944

Dear Minna, Janey, Mary, and Cornelia:

Well, here I am again, home safe and unsound. I lay around the Algonquin until train time, while Helen shopped for birthday presents for Rosie and an evening dress for herself to keep up her mo-

Lunch time again

rale. She tells people that I was sick in the house of my girl, her mother, and sisters. "Well, now nice," say the neighbors primly.

The porter on our train finally showed up after I had dropped the big suitcase in the aisle and Helen had carried it the rest of the way. He was a very old man and asked us to call him at six. Seems he oversleeps.

We were only twenty minutes late, owing to the engineer, who had belladonna in his eyes. The conductor was a pleasant little man who had never made this run before and had the feeling he was going backward.

At Grand Central we could not get a cab till Helen told a redcap I had pneumonia. "Oh, I'll get your father a cab right away," he said, and he did.

The porter woke by himself, I forgot to say. "How are you, George?" he said. "Morning, boss," I said.

September 22

A kind of moribundity got me yesterday after so much exercise with a pencil. I feel stronger today — I could easily crack an English walnut.

Yesterday was hot and muggy like a fifteen-year-old Pekinese, but today is beautiful, clear, sunny, C major. . . .

JIM

◄◄►►

West Cornwall,
Connecticut
June 29, 1950

Dear Ronnie and Janey:

We celebrated Helen's birthday last night with two bottles of Hemingway's favorite champagne and other liquids, not forgetting frequent toasts to you and the new daughter. We are anxious to hear all the details, complete with a description of the new beauty.

We had a wonderful time at Kenyon with Tom Matthews,[1] who made a remarkably fine commencement address and with whom we started what looks like a firm friendship. We are going to spend a weekend at his house in Rhode Island about the middle of August and sometime during that month *Time* is going to run a cover story about Jamie Thurber, the artist from Columbus, who draws with his feet. Naturally, we talked a great deal about the Williamses. Tom seems to have gained something unusual in spiritual stature from the long illness of his wife,[2] who must have been a very great lady. I will send you a copy of his address when I get one, since there is so much in it that you would understand.

I am mailing my *Bermudian* piece,[3] . . . and I'm sorry it will be a few days late, but I got back late from Ohio with an enormous amount of work to do. I got through the four-hour ceremony without falling down and have a hood to show for it in purple and white satin like the lining of a United States senator's coffin. The weather was wonderful and the people were lovely. When we get settled down Helen and I will both write in greater detail. *The 13 Clocks* is coming along fine.

What name did you finally decide on?

Love and kisses to all
of you from

THE THURBERS

1. T. S. Matthews, editor of *Time* magazine.
2. Juliana Cuyler Matthews, his first wife.
3. Williams had regained the editorship (though not the ownership) of *The Bermudian*.

◄◄►►

West Cornwall,
Connecticut
December 15, 1951

Dear Ronnie:

. . . *The New Yorker* may be financially rich, but it has become terribly poor with the death of Ross. This was a shocking blow to all of us, and I find it hard to throw off. We had seen him several times recently and were greatly worried. He had known since about May that it was cancer, but he believed that it was being cured by new deep radium treatment. We are not sure, but apparently the doctors were not aware that it was deep and extensive until the operation. The part they were clearing up turned out to be small. He died without coming out of the anesthetic. We were telephoned at 10:30 that night. Gibbs practically collapsed, but Andy wrote the obituary while I stood by that long and awful day. Five hundred people turned up at his funeral, at which a reverend who didn't know him intoned stuff that Ross would have hated and rolled his r's. As White said, there were wakes in a hundred bars that night.

Everybody keeps asking if the magazine will go on, and it will. Lobrano and Shawn have been getting it out alone most of this year, and they have been doing the buying of pieces longer than that. He suffered no great pain, but was bothered and kept awake by constant coughing. He lived alone at the Algonquin, where we saw him a lot. On his last birthday we gave him a scarf and called on him, and I had dinner with him that week. When I called him and said "Happy Birthday," he said, "Thanks, old fellow," and then, "Goddam it, when Forster[1] phoned me and said it was my birthday, I knew you would be calling up." He had worried for years about his friends dying in their fifties, especially Woollcott, Benchley, Broun, and MacNamara.

The day after he died, I showed Andy a drawing of mine showing my dog lying at the end of a grave and staring at the headstone. He was all for using it as the illustration for the obituary, but the

---

1. Louis Forster, Ross's assistant.

conservative boys turned it down. Now Andy and I have made a pledge to use it for the obituary of whichever one of us dies first. I will either write his, or he will write mine. I'm going to do a piece about Ross, but it will take time. He was the principal figure in my career, and I don't know what I would have amounted to without his magazine, in which ninety percent of my stuff has appeared. He was also a great part of my life, and I realize how much I loved him and depended on him. There was no appreciation quite the same as his, because it was all tied up with him and his life. What White and I did was a part of the guy, and we realize how much of our work was done with him in mind. For the first time I have become deeply aware of the chill sweeping across the cold and starry space. I felt it when Herman Miller died, but I saw him only once every few years, and Ross was a part of my daily life for almost exactly a quarter of a century. It is always hard to believe that extremely vital people can die. He represented life to me the way only a few others do. These include you and Janey. Take care of yourselves, and, as Ross said a thousand times, God bless you.

And a Merry Christmas from us all.

As ever,

J$_{IM}$

‹‹››

West Cornwall,
Connecticut
July 31, 1952

Dear Janey and, ah there, old boy!

I am now convinced that last Sunday's *Male Animal*[1] was the sloppiest ever put on, and I'm sorry Janey had to see that one. Elliott was thinking about my *Times* piece and left out lines. At the end of Act One he should say, "Rah! Rah! Rah! Ferguson! Ferguson! Ferguson!" but he forgot the three Fergusons. The line he missed in the floppy-blue-hat scene holds the scene together. "Maybe I ought to go," says Joe, and Tommy says, "Oh, no! You're not exactly a stranger around here." Elliott scrabbled through the scene and brought up five different lines instead. Everybody else was way off, too. . . . This play depends on audience and actors together, and the Sunday audience was a basket lunch crowd out of the Bronx and Des Moines. Gus Lobrano went one crowded Friday night and said, "It was wonderful, the audience stood and cheered after the play, and I was sure it's going to run eight years." I thought the first act was good only because these automatons got through it like poodles walking on their hind legs. You applaud, but you're damn glad when it's over.

Both Nugents, like all perceptive people, thought Janey was wonderful, and when I talked to Elliott Tuesday he said, "Aren't we going to see any more of Mrs. Williams?" I know you must be glad I restrained myself this time from crying "Help! Fire! Police!" before the plane took off. The radar at Idlewild had been picking up some funny things in the skies recently, and I do hope you all three got to see a luminous yellow visitor from Mars drifting past the plane.

As I told Elliott, Janey's visits are like those of flying saucers. People see her shining brightly for a moment and then she is gone, and some doubt there actually *is* one. We got back last night at six, and Helen put the last drop of cortisone in my eye at midnight,

---

1. The revival of *The Male Animal*, again starring Elliott Nugent, had a longer run than the original production.

with her backhand. She has a good drop shot on both wings after long practice twelve years ago. Dr. Bruce said I had a close call, but that I am now out of the woods. He does not expect rational behavior from writers, though, even when they cut their eye open with a handkerchief. He vouchsafed the information that the membrane which makes my eye look like a dropped poached egg is twice as thick as it was, but I'm not worried. It means that girls will have to wear dresses twice as yellow as they were two years ago, if I am to chase and catch them, but there will always be some light to see by.

Helen just came in with two objects my mother sent us two years ago, a vase made from the casing of a French 75 shell which I bought at Fort Douaumont in 1918, and which is about as pretty as a universal joint; and an earthenware vase, hand-painted by my mother about 1886, the year the first Sherlock Holmes story was written. This vase is shaped like a hot-water bottle, and when Helen handed it to me, I said, "I thought these things were different than they used to be." The flowers and the birds on the thing are set off by a background I can only call prison-pallor gray. When older women hear about Janey's breakfast of four peppermints and five cigarettes, they turn the same gray and cry, "There are no things that age can give like those it takes away." Ronnie will probably see the flaw in this quote, but in its words and not its sense. . . .

There are still people standing in line to meet Janey, including Honey,[2] with whom we had lunch Tuesday. She is as gray as a badger, but Helen says her face has become kindly, as remarkable a change as if I became a strong silent man, and Ronnie went around lecturing on the virtues of moderation in everything.

Love and kisses from my little family to your big family.

As ever,

JIM

2. Writer Ann Honeycutt, one of Thurber's early flames.

West Cornwall,
Connecticut
May 29, 1953

Dear Janey:

I always wanted to buy an abandoned railway station myself, and there is a most adorable one at Taconic, Connecticut, which I could get for $27,500. It is complete with iron stove, leather chair with broken springs, and a 1932 calendar on the wall. That was the year everything closed down.

There must be a merry-go-round somewhere, and I will try to merry-go-find it for you. The *New Yorker* boys can check, but they'll probably ask me if you'll settle for a Ferris wheel, or a 1905 football stadium. The merry-go-rounds I knew in Columbus were as big as a good-sized living room and would probably be worth a lot of money now as museum pieces. I haven't seen one in years, or decades. There is a kind of children's carousel that I used to see in the gardens of Paris that children can ride on and that is only as big as a good-sized bathroom, but I don't think we have any over here. How about a nice 1900 hurdy-gurdy? I will see what I can find out about merry-go-rounds, no kidding. I think you meant calliope when you said "carousel," but whether you could get a steam organ with a modern merry-go-round, I don't know. . . .

Don't get your hopes too high about the merry-go-round, since a good secondhand one ought to cost about $22,000 and shipping would probably bring the price up to $30,000. How about a small mountain range, lady? We have some lovely mountain ranges. Love and kisses to all of you from both of us.

As ever,

JIM

Janey is contemplating her fifth child and Dr. Thurber is worried.

◄◄►►

West Cornwall,
Connecticut
December 6, 1954

Dearest children:

I just finished a letter to Rosie telling her that Jane, who was pregnant when Rosie was one, is still keeping up with her. I explained that "six," which sounds like "sex" in English, sounds like "cease" in French, and that this should be remembered. All mothers feel chummy about other mothers, but Rosie had hoped to have next April to herself, never dreaming that our adopted child in Bermuda would try to beat my grandmother's record of six children in twenty-five years. Of course, we send you our love and best wishes first of all, before reminding you two of certain well-established statistics and a few I just thought up myself. Having a child at forty-three is considered de rigueur by the medicos, although a little rigorous on the cervix, the budget, and the aging father. He will be about sixty when his coming child is ten. If, at that time, 1965, Ronald should be taken by our Heavenly Father in the fifth set of a match with the old Commander, it is unlikely that even the most worshipful and eligible male would care to take on a ready-made family of such size, and I abhor the idea of Janey toying with the notion of going into the deluxe white-slave trade that glitters between New York and Buenos Aires. . . .

Since I'll be sixty day after tomorrow — without a child of ten — I'm old enough to be skeptical of a pregnancy resulting from menstruation, but Fritzi[1] has just told me she knows of such cases — one mother didn't realize her pregnancy until she got kicked in the stomach. I once read in a medical book this unconsciously sardonic sentence: "Precautionary measures are never infallible and one

1. Thurber's secretary, Elfride (von) Kuegelgen.

should not be cocksure about any contraceptive." It is easy to see which one the author meant. Dr. Thurber, on this subject, recently stated: "Being careful ninety-nine times out of a hundred isn't often enough." This learned layman and conclusion-jumper is inclined to lay the delicate condition at the door, or in the bed, of celebration — that is, to blame it on merrymaking of the kind that creeps up on a couple in the night when snug seems more important than safe.

This business of every four years that Janey speaks of, and women do have cycles, would bring number 7 when Janey is forty-seven, and somebody should put his foot down on that number, or keep his pants buttoned, or something. Dr. Damon,[2] among the best obstetricians in the world today, terminates pregnancies after the age of forty-four, a practice followed by all reputable medical men. I am naturally a little worried about barefoot white-collared doctors who cannot tell one rash from another, are puzzled by high temperatures, take blood pressure rather than pulse, in hunting for factor X, and are inclined to massage the prostate rather than feel the thyroid in cases of galloping toxicity. The effect of climate on professional judgments in any field has been studied by the proper authorities, and a woman of forty-seven, married to a virile Man-o'-War, retired to stud, should look for certain signs in her doctors' demeanor. If they have given up wearing collars or shaving, can't remember names and dates, and confuse the advisability of pregnancy with that of having another highball, the hopefully unexpectant mother should demand a change of venue, or consider separate beds, or the desirability of sending her husband to Denmark, where, as Victor Borge says, "We have three sexes — male, female, and convertible." I'm not talking about Bermuda doctors we all know, for they will have joined their colleagues in heaven when Janey is fifty-four and still going strong. I'm worried about the advice she may get at that time from God-knows-who. The oldest mother in American medical records was fifty-seven, and I ask God to reinforce my prayerful conviction that the Williamses do not intend to aim at her record. She was a mountain woman without shoes except the one she lived in with all her young (see Mother Goose).

2. Dr. Virgil Damon, who delivered Thurber's daughter.

We have three bottles of Pol Roget which we decided not to contribute to a birthday party being given for me by Rose tomorrow night. I told Helen I want to keep at least one bottle for Ronnie's alteration party. This is a simple operation, not to be confused with emasculation, for it is merely a tying off exactly comparable to a woman's. Anyway, somebody has to do something before two A.M. of, say, December 25, 1958, after the Zuills[3] have gone home with the other guests and Ronnie is sitting alone in the living room drinking and glinting and comforting himself with the belief that it's a lot of nonsense to drive all the way to Hamilton for what Peaches Browning once referred to in court as "one of those things." Anyway, the pharmacy would be closed. "The hell with it, we haven't run out of girls' names yet, and there's the plaguey hundredth chance nothing will happen."

I will close with a few offhand suggestions: the wife can always lock the bedroom door. By the time he has broken it down, he ought to be worn out, at sixty. And by that time Lane Bryant may have put in a supply of perfectly darling chastity belts. There is always Denmark, to be sure, but I hesitate to recommend a mixed-doubles game in which the wife accidentally deflowers her mate with a well-directed forehand smash. The trouble with Ronnie is not that he has two strikes on him, but I will not labor the point. Something ought to be done with it though. Meanwhile, I send all of you my love and best wishes for a Merry Christmas, a happy blessed event, and a sane 1958. . . .

<small>GRANDPA</small>

3. An elderly Bermudian couple versed in the island's history.

◄◄►►

Stafford Hotel
London, England
June 23, 1955

Dearest family:

Tonight we are having dinner with Tom and Martha Matthews,[1] and there will be both English and Americans present, including Dick Watts[2] and John Hayward, T. S. Eliot's friend and roommate. I have been on television with the editor of *Punch*, and we must have had at least twenty dinner parties or cocktail parties. I will enclose the best of the interviews, written by a man on the *Daily Mail*. . . .

There seems to be something about England that keeps its writers alive to a ripe old age, and we are thinking of settling down here. One of my English friends is going to take me to meet Walter de la Mare, who is eighty-two, but I won't be able to meet Max Beerbohm, eighty-three, since he is in Italy. . . . Eden Phillpots is now writing for television at the age of ninety-two, and today's *Times* notes that H. M. Tomlinson celebrated his eighty-second birthday yesterday, quietly, at home. In America, as you know, most male writers fail to reach the age of sixty, or, if they do, they have nothing more to say, but occasionally say it anyway.

At one party I met J. B. Priestley again, just after he had done his weekly television show consisting of half-a-dozen skits, which he not only writes, but also appears in as actor. He was sixty years old last September and is still going strong.

Sir Laurence Olivier is doing *Macbeth* at Stratford, and I have an idea of writing a piece about the old tragedy, disagreeing with the modern interpretations. It seems that Sir Laurence puts a great deal of beauty into Macbeth's single sentence, after he learns the news that Lady Macbeth has died. The line is: "She should have died hereafter." The Thurber version of this line gives it an impatient note and I think that I am on sound ground here not only as a

---

1. T. S. Matthews's second wife, Martha Gellhorn (who was previously married to Hemingway).

2. Richard Watts, dramatic critic of the *New York Herald Tribune*.

Lady Macbeth

student of *Macbeth* but as a husband of many years' experience. My feeling is that Macbeth had plenty on his hands the way it was — what with a forest moving in on him, to say nothing of the fact that everything else had gone wrong from the beginning — and I feel that he blamed most of his misfortune on his wife. No other scholar I know of has pointed out that Lady Macbeth is one of the few female sleep-talkers in fiction. My studies have shown that for every woman that talks in her sleep, there are 130 husbands; and what Lady Macbeth did was to involve her husband seriously by blabbing his guilt through echoing corridors. People who walk in their sleep never talk, and it may be that Macbeth simply imagined that she was giving him away.

In any case, I expect someday to do my own version of the play, although I am pretty sure it will not be in England. It must be remembered that it was Lady Macbeth who suggested killing the King in her own castle, and I pointed out in *The New Yorker* last year that the place to kill a king is on a heath, not in your own home. Macbeth finished off Banquo outdoors at night, and the fact that Ronnie and I have finished off many a guest of ours inside the house at Seaforth proves nothing. . . .

We command you to write us a letter here at the Stafford Hotel, where we will be for at least another three weeks.

Love and kisses from us both to all nine or ten of you.

As ever,

JIM

◄◄◊►►

Stafford Hotel
London, England
August 4, 1955

Dear Ronnie:

Every week or so over here some viscount has his license taken away for driving while full of port. Most of these chaps no longer care what happens, and one of them told the magistrate that he didn't give a good god damn. He had to pay a fine and the court costs, since not giving a good god damn is not regarded as sufficient excuse. If you can actually turn over and over in a ditch with your wife and seven children and all of you come out unhurt,[1] you can easily sell the act to Ringling Brothers, under the name of The Nine Flying Williamses — come on in and see them, folks, they do not give a good god damn. I want you to pull yourself together, for you have a good eight to ten years left of life if you will behave. . . .

The Loch Ness story has turned out to be endlessly fascinating. I hope you can get hold of two books by Lt. Commander R. T. Gould, but they are both out of print. One is called *The Loch Ness Monster and Others*, and the other, published earlier, *The Case for the Sea Serpent.* Gould leaves no doubt in my mind that there are sea serpents and that there is a creature of that species, or its cousin, in Loch Ness. But this is a long story which you will read later. Gould shows, by actual evidence, that sea serpents have been seen and reported in logs by some British officers now of the highest rank in the navy or maritime service. He also traces some beautiful monster stories as far back as one that appeared off Gloucester, Massachusetts, in 1817–19. Now it sticks in my mind, old fellow, that you once told me about sighting a sea serpent — either yourself or a friend of yours saw it, along with his crew. Or you may have been quoting some of the witnesses Gould mentions. I couldn't see him because he died two years ago. . . .

You now owe us about three letters. Please share our love with

---

1. The Williamses had been involved in a minor automobile accident.

your wee wifie and your innumerable offspring and come across with the name of the youngest, even if it *is* Lavinia.

Gin up! Sober to the Wheel! Sherry on!

Love and kisses,

JIM

◄◄◇►

West Cornwall,
Connecticut
August 27, 1960

Dear Children:

   . . . We went to Central City, Colorado, where our *Carnival*[1]
played all of August at the old opera house. It was a trip into the
past. The town has a crier with cowbells and there are not many
baths or telephones. It's 8500 feet high, and I was one of the few
not affected by the altitude. It got Helen's sinus a little. So we spent
our last two weeks at the Brown Palace Hotel in Denver, the most
wonderful and luxurious hotel in the world. Denver is full of rich
widows who give parties around their swimming pools. The
women are most friendly, and instead of shaking hands hug you.
One young lady said to me, late at night, "I don't wear any stock-
ings — see?" I told her I couldn't see, and she said, "Well, feel
then." The next minute she was in Helen's lap.

   We got back to New York August 22, Dorothy Parker's sixty-
seventh birthday. My first love, Eva Rosebud Prout Barks Geiger,
will be sixty-six in October. On our way back we stopped in Chicago to meet my son-in-law's parents for the first time. We had
lunch with them and Rosie and Fred,[2] and Sara, aged six, and Gre-
gory, aged four, but able to take a house apart in half an hour. The
youngest, Mark, nine months, is said to be a genius, because he
can darn near walk and talk, and looks a little like the Great Quil-
low.[3] I didn't walk till I was five or talk till I was seven. Rosie is
getting over a slight case of postpartum jitters and I have had a
spooky feeling for a long while, but it is going away.

   Helen is fine and she has been the balance wheel of the *Carnival*
company since the beginning, the only one who can deal with all
the different egos. When one actor threatened to quit, his wife
wrote him, "Don't you do anything till you talk it over with Mrs.
Thurber." He didn't quit. The show broke all records out there by

---

   1. *A Thurber Carnival*, the review in which Thurber later acted in eighty-eight performances
on Broadway.
   2. Frederick W. Sauers — Rosemary's husband, father of Thurber's three grandchildren.
   3. The tiny hero of Thurber's fairy tale of the same name.

"You're going a bit far, Miss Blanchard."

selling out for the whole month in advance, and we even had to put on three extra performances. It grossed $164,000, or about twice as much as the next highest, Lillian Hellman's *The Lark*. It reopens at the ANTA Labor Day matinee.

As ever,

JIM

THE
THURBER CIRCLE

Thurber and his Circle.

Advice to Wolcott Gibbs during rehearsals of Gibbs's play, Season in the Sun, *before it was produced in 1950:*

‹‹◊›

West Cornwall,
Connecticut
Summer 1950

Dear Wolcott:

. . . As a man who has crossed the Gobi Desert, I feel the Christian desire to point out some familiar terrors that you will have to endure. . . . If you have Maney[1] you avoid a lot of this, but Maney is likely to phone your wife, the way he phoned Helen from Princeton, and growl, "Stay where you are. Only one funny scene." He had watched dress rehearsal with six other guys wearing hats and overcoats and smoking cigars. One of the actors fumbled every line and kept saying "Balls," so that fifteen speeches ended with this word. It was the night before opening and we had to cut twenty lines from the first act; sitting up too late; drinking too much; eating too little. There was the usual last-hour panic. Shumlin wanted to put spectacles on the villain to make him comic and Nugent wanted to put his father into the part. Someone had quietly rewritten the charm out of the dancing scene and it had lines like "What do you say we shake a leg?" . . .

You can't expect to have your second-act curtain until the night before you hit Broadway. You are certain that two actors are going to get tonsillitis and you are likely to demand a run-through at quarter to seven. Meredith's[2] girls are pretty sure to put lines in your play and so is the producer's secretary and a middle-aged woman in brown you never identify. Some of these lines are good and they stay in.

During rehearsal you discover that your prettiest lines do not cross the footlights, because they are too pretty, or an actor can't

1. Richard Maney, press agent for *The Male Animal.*
2. Burgess Meredith, who later directed *A Thurber Carnival,* was directing Gibbs's play.

say them, or an actress doesn't know what they mean. There comes the horrible realization that phrases like "Yes you were" or "No I won't" are better and more effective than the ones you slaved over; especially the ones that survived the eleventh rewrite. On the thirteenth day of rehearsal, the play suddenly makes no sense to you and does not seem to be written in English. You wonder why you wrote it and have a wild intention to ask the producer to postpone it a year. In this state you are likely to fall into the orchestra pit or find yourself taking an actress to Jackson Heights in a cab. She will praise Benchley and Perelman and ask you if you believe there are people in real life like those in *Tobacco Road*. You will only have a twenty-dollar bill and she will pay the cab. Your wife will wonder until she dies why you had to take the girl home and why you don't know more about the play if you attended every rehearsal. . . .

On the opening night in New York you will decide not to see the show, but you will; standing in the rear, expecting doorknobs to come loose, lights not to light, entrances not to be made, and actors to put in new lines. You will remember W. H. Davies's "What is life then, if we cannot stand and stare like sheep and cows?" None of these things will happen, but you will go out for a drink when the scene comes up that never was done right in rehearsal or out of town. — It will be done perfectly. Some actress will tell you, at the bar, that she always gets diarrhea on opening night because all actresses do. You will then decide to watch the second act backstage and guys you haven't seen before will call you "Mack" and "Buddy" and push you around. Watch out that you don't pick up an important prop from the prop table and forget what you did with it. Don't walk through any door, or you will find yourself on the stage. . . . Doors of dressing rooms should be left ajar, since actresses can close them in such a way that it takes a carpenter to get them open.

At the beginning of the third act you will be appalled by the fact that everyone is whispering and that the crosses have been slowed down. You will then be sure that they are doing the first act over again. This is because of third-act eardrum, which makes everything sound dim and causes important lines to sound like "Did you find the foursome in the two green bags?" It is now time to go to the bar again, where you will find a large man in a tuxedo, who walked out on the play. He will tell you that he hasn't sat all the way through a show since *The Lion and the Mouse.* You will get back to the theatre in time to see Dick Watts running for his typewriter. He will say something to you that sounds like "Organ recital; vested fever." You will not be able to mingle with the people coming out; the best thing is to go bravely backstage; but at this point you are on your own. Whatever happens, avoid Marc Connelly. He told Nugent that we had given Brahms' Fifth to a man with a mandolin. Fortunately for us, there isn't any Brahms' Fifth. This is the only real comfort I can give you. Best of luck and God bless you.

J<small>IM</small>

Gibbs was about to go into the newspaper business on Fire Island.

◄◄►►

Waterville Inn
Paget East, Bermuda
May 21, 1954

Dear Wolcott:

I have never got out a country or island newspaper, but I have sat around in bars with a lot of other ex-newspapermen who dreamily talked of either getting out such a newspaper in their fifties or of divorcing their wives, both difficult and ill-advised projects. I was editor of my college daily, the *Ohio State Lantern,* back in 1917–18, and seven years later I was assistant editor of the Riviera edition of the *Chicago Tribune.* Editing these papers was something like playing a cross-eyed left-handed woman tennis player. You never know where anything is coming from, and everything takes a queer bounce. My only achievements on these papers consisted of little feats of technical ingenuity. In college I was forever throwing a dead-head Lucky Strike ad, about half the size of a welcome mat, into the paper to fill up space. On the Riviera edition I borrowed large cuts from the French Bureau of Tourisme and kept dropping them in when copy was scarce. Once, when three or four columns were still left vacant, I set the whole damn paper up in 10-point. This may have been the only 10-point issue of a paper ever got out, I don't know. I do know the Riviera edition folded for good at the end of that season.

When I ran out of front-page news in college, I would write an editorial, between midnight and two A.M., and set it in a four-column box near the bottom of page one. I was a slow headline writer, even after long practice, and with nothing more difficult to deal with than number-one heads with an easy letter count of 12 to 14 — both papers had the same count. The college Linotyper used to come in at two in the morning and say, "What are you doing, trying to make them headlines rhyme?" I worked so long on heads that I forgot to bother about news and I rarely had enough.

"Look out, Harry!"

Since I was also a legman in Nice, I would sometimes go back and expand stories I had already written and headed up, once adding two columns to my bewildering account of the Wills–Lenglen tennis match.[1] Of this account John Tunis[2] later said, "It betrayed no knowledge whatever of tennis, but a considerable grasp of women." Sometimes I threw my integrity to the winds and made up stories. In Nice one night I invented a British colonel and his wife who had taken a villa on Cap d'Antibes and who owned a champion blue Angora cat, whose cups and ribbons I described in detail. I think I reported not long ago in *The New Yorker*, another weekly that makes me nervous, how I was saved in college one night by the fortuitous appearance in the night skies of the most brilliant aurora borealis seen in Ohio since the Civil War. You have

---

1. France's Suzanne Lenglen defeated Helen Wills of the U.S.A. in a famous match at Cannes.
2. A sportswriter for *The New Yorker*.

to have a lot of luck like that. Once, when the late Don Skene forgot a promise to phone me the news of some big American event in Cannes, I went out into the streets at midnight to flag down all cars coming from the direction of that city. The first one I stopped was full of the men who had taken part in this event, whatever it was.

You will not, of course, be handicapped the way I was in southern France by printers who speak only Niçois, a kind of patois that sounds like French spoken in a nightmare. But since your typewriter keyboard has the same mischievous proximity of *s* and *d* as mine had, you will have to be careful that the brilliant deductions of your island constabulary do not become seductions. You will also have to get used to continual visits from all the unbalanced people on the island, who love to plague editors. Our most constant night visitor in Nice was not unbalanced, but he was so diverting that we often didn't get the paper out till dawn when he dropped in. I mean the late, wonderful Frank Harris, with his endless recollections of Wilde, Shaw, Hardy, and all the others. Gene Fowler or John O'Hara could conceivably keep you up till dawn, but they are a little young and shy to be as diverting as old Harris.

I trust that you managed to get on your exchange list the invaluable and truly marvelous *Newtown Bee,* of Connecticut. I haven't seen the *Bee* for years, but when I lived near Newtown twenty years ago it was a big, floppy, endless journal filled with wonderful announcements, such as that of a forthcoming "imitation tennis tournament"; and it often published long letters from its readers about their visits abroad, one of which contained, in a lengthy discussion of Notre Dame cathedral, this enlightening little fact: "Gargoyles are water sports."

I am glad I am not in your shoes, your desk, and your eyeshade. With sixty staring me in the face, I have developed inflammation of the sentence structure and a definite hardening of the paragraphs. You and your staff have all my sincere best wishes and your good wife has all of my deepest consolations. You will have to call her in to help from time to time, as I called my own wife to help in Nice. This is a good idea, because wives get things done when husbands give up. Be sure you check the dateline before putting the paper to bed and let me know if you ever learn to read type backward after you have locked up the forms. I could never do that. At least you won't be challenged by an armed sentry on the way home from your office at night, the way I was when I crossed the Ohio State campus. I always halted promptly when he cried "Halt!" I sometimes have my moments of depression when I wish I hadn't.

As always,

JIM

P.S. The Paris edition of the *Chicago Tribune*, no longer extant, was a country newspaper published in a great city. We got only fifty words of cable each night and the city editor would take sentences out of this cable and pass them around the desk to Bill Shirer, Elliot Paul, and me, saying "Write a column on that." I shall always remember two sentences he handed me. One of them was, "Christy Mathewson died tonight at Saranac." The other said simply, "Admiral Richard E. Byrd flew to the North Pole and back in seventeen and a half hours."

◄◄►►

New York City
February 8, 1956

Dear Wolcott:

I'm writing this in my office in *The New Yorker,* through whose corridors, *Time* magazine said fifteen years ago, I often walked, an aged gray-eyed respected ghost. The aged and gray are still true, but it's hard to tell around here about respect anymore, or its kindred feelings. Ross used to send a note reading, "Jesus Christ, that was a swell piece." All you get now, if you insist on finding out what happened to a manuscript, is a telegram saying, "Piece bought, money deposited." A month ago they rejected a casual of mine with the highest and warmest and most complete praise I have got since Ross died. Things have come to a pretty pass if we are going to have to write rejections, as Tom Gorman[1] calls them.

I'm going to have Miss Terry send you the new directory of personnel in the Business Department. I didn't realize that we have jolly representatives not only in all the major cities of America, but in Europe, too, with a few regional operatives thrown in, such as the man who represents us in "Pittsburgh and Ohio." . . .

It seems to me that you should show up around here at least once a year to break the legend now becoming firmly established that no one is allowed in your office and that it remains exactly as you left it the last time you were here — the copy of the *New York Times* lying carelessly in a chair, the little clock on the desk stopped, the coffee cup from Schrafft's still partly filled with the coffee of 1953 or whenever it was. Anybody can get in my office and frequently asks me what I want when I come in. One of the last times I saw Ross, less than a year before he died, he said something that I keep remembering and wondering about. We were coming back from the Algonquin and, with his great frown and pendulous tongue dominating the street scene, he suddenly said, "Oh, well, you can always write for the theatre." I told this to White yesterday and he said, "He made no such provisions for me."

1. A *New Yorker* secretary.

I wish we could have seen you earlier and longer last Thursday night. Love and kisses —

As always,

JIM

◄◄◇►

New York City
May 2, 1946

Dear Tommy: [1]

You can imagine my surprise when I learned that Ralph Hodgson is not only alive, but living in Minerva, Ohio. My wife, who is certainly not Scarlet and only the slightest touch gray, read me that William Rose Benét (who is not to be confused with Billy Rose Benét, the producer) is going to present a medal to Hodgson, not so much because of his exalted achievements in poetry, I gather, as because of the extraordinary and unique fact that he is living in Minerva, Ohio. I had no idea that Hodgson had outlived Swinburne, the last of the famous poets of the British 1890s, who died in 1909. There is something abut a poet which leads us to believe that he died, in many cases, as long as twenty years before his birth. I often win as much as $5.00 at literary gatherings by betting modern poets and teachers of English, or middle-aged ladies who have had too much Madeira and have started to explain T. S. Eliot to some engineer in a corner, that they cannot come within ten years of the year Swinburne died. The closest anyone has ever come was 1900, and the engineer I am talking about, a graduate of O.S.U., 1931, picked 1878 as the date of Algernon's demise.

To get back to Hodgson, the fact that he is living in Minerva, Ohio, is just as astounding to me as if I'd been told that Ernie Dowson was playing left field on the Newark Bears, or that William Ernest Henley had been made the new managing editor of *Butterick Patterns.* Just like you, I have always associated Hodgson with the period of Whistler and Degas. This is possibly because his most famous poems, such as "Eve" and "The Bull," have the classic form and beauty which we associate only with things that were produced long before John Wilce. It is interesting to note at this point that although Elliott Nugent, Henry Fonda, and James Bell, all playing in *The Male Animal,* said to their respective Ellens, "Have you ever read Hodgson's poem 'The Bull'?," none of them was ever interested enough to find a copy of Ralph's poems and read this wonderful set of verses. This is because of what is known as "the pace

---

1. Thomas Meek, Thurber's broker, who had been an O.S.U. classmate.

of American life." I think it was the great Joe Taylor[2] who first introduced me to "Eve" with a berry halfway to her lips. "Mr. Thurber," he said, "this is Ralph Hodgson's girl friend Eve." Through Joe Taylor I met, among others, Joseph Conrad and Henry James and A. E. Housman. There have been a great many false rumors as to what actually happened at that wonderful party so many years ago.

And in my autobiography *I Outlived Them All*, chapter three is given over to a bold and vivid description, not to say confession, of every single thing that took place. The news that Hodgson is still alive will of course force me to postpone the publication of the book. My publishers, a nervous and haunted group of gentlemen, have been insisting for years that I probably have *not* outlived them all, and Mr. Mifflin has protested since 1914 that Ambrose Bierce would show up some day and flatly refute every single thing I have written about the amazing quadrangle that existed among Hodgson, Conrad, Nugent, and Eve.

As an employee of the Department of Agriculture in the days when A. P. Sandals invented the deathless motto "The rainbow comes down in Ohio" (abandoned at the request of the Better Business Bureau in 1928), I used to travel all over the state carrying diamond-shaped placards advertising the Ohio State Fair. In this way I visited such little-known places as Dilly's Bottom, a charming and idyllic little corner of obscurity, half of whose residents believed that Franklin Delano Roosevelt and Theodore Roosevelt were one and the same man. The other fifty percent of the town's inhabitants have been hiding out in the nearby woods since the appearance of Halley's comet in 1910. As you remember, this famous comet almost hit the earth that time, and so frightened Mark Twain that he died. This mysterious heavenly visitor is due again in 1985, at which time there is every likelihood the earth will be completely destroyed, I hope. This is not as bad as it would have been in 1910, because in 1985 only turtle life will be left on the planet because of the atom bomb and other engines of war even more horrific. . . .

> *Sincere greetings*
> *and best wishes,*
>
> JIM

2. Joseph Russell Taylor, Thurber's favorite English professor at O.S.U.

‑‑◇►►

West Cornwall,
Connecticut
July 18, 1952

Dear Ted and Julia:[1]

I was never in Europe for less than fourteen months at a time, but I met a lot of Americans, usually Middle Westerners, who were trying to see Europe at sixty miles an hour. They remind me of the two young Phi Psi's I met in 1934 who had driven from New York to Columbus in ten hours. An Ohio woman said to me in Carcassonne, "We saw all there is to see in Provence last Sunday afternoon."

It's nice to have children and grandchildren if you don't tell them anything about the way we all acted from college up to now, or last November for you. Don't sing them, "Put on your old gray bonnet . . . and we'll hitch old Dobbin to the sleigh." Be honest and sing, "Put on your old cloche hat and we'll drive the old Marmon into the Indianola Park swimming pool." We can't outrun our past or stare it out of countenance in the living room after the kids have gone home. You've got to take up a hobby to forget that spaniel and the heartbreak you had when you found out that Theta's have cold feet and that your friends lose their charm and brilliance when you quit looking at them through the bottom of a glass. We tie spaniels to railroad tracks and are afraid of the cops. I suggest reading books, playing checkers, taking up painting, or collecting old magazines and sheet music. Don't go in for religion, or count up to ten thousand, or throw cards into a hat. That would be using the same part of the mind that has got you where you are. Where are you? I keep thinking of Don Casto not smoking on the maiden voyage of that goddam zeppelin. The strange desire to get on a thing that has never been tried out puzzles me, but then I remember the Titanic better than you do. When you and Julia get on the first rocket to the moon you're going to have to make the trip with the Castos and you'll just have to get used to the idea. A friend of mine

1. F. R. Gardiner and his wife Julia, old friends in Columbus, who were mourning the loss of a pet dog.

who packed all his frustrations, regrets, and dreams into the love of an English setter had an extremely wise and cunning wife. When the dog died, she had it stuffed with its fangs showing and its eyes bloodshot, and there was a mechanism inside the thing. When her husband touched the dog, it not only snapped at him but squirted water on him. This guy is now president of the Dog Catchers' Association.

If you can still spell, why don't you play the word game? I was going to send you a pack of playing cards, but if you're too old to lay them on the table, they won't do you any good. Elliott asked me on the phone why you didn't show up at the theatre, and I couldn't persuade him that you were sensible about it. It takes your mind off things and you must not give up wanting that. Why don't you strike up a friendship with my brother William? His heart was broken by the death of our bull terrier Rex, the defeat of Teddy Roosevelt in 1912, and the retirement from the movies of J. Warren Kerrigan. As for me, I don't even weep for Adonaïs. I got work to do. Blessings on you both.

As ever,

Jᴉᴍ

P.S. You should know that no dog likes to die in the presence of human beings, or under anybody's bed. It is a profound instinct in that species which makes it want to die alone and not with all its relatives around the bed. An old brown poodle up here crept away and hid in autumn leaves almost identically his own color, but he was found and dragged back home. This is a true and terrible story. It is probable that a dog would kill itself to avoid the kind of death it abhors.

◄◄►►

West Cornwall,
Connecticut
November 3, 1952

Dear old Frank:[1]

I didn't actually reach Admissions, although I had thought I would have to stay all night for a basal. It turns out that this test is inaccurate and undependable and perhaps even touched by fantasy — "You get funny numbers," Dr. Parsons told me, "like eighteen." It seems that high blood pressure, for example, will make a normal metabolism rate seem high — the body, you see, doesn't know its veins from a gland in the neck. I swallowed a couple of Lily-cupsful of radioactive iodine, which looks and tastes exactly like water, and the next day I came back and lay down under a Geiger counter. They allow you as high as 45 percent in this new measurement, and are urgently concerned only if you reach 75. I did 56, which is a funny number, but not so terrible. I will take four pills a day for fourteen to eighteen months, and then see if I can get along without them. Fifty percent of people do, which is what I call the American Odds: fifty–fifty, heads and tails, six of one and half a dozen of the other, you go your way and I'll go mine, and so on. *Moitié-moitié,* too, or one lark to one horse. I'm supposed to begin to feel better in a few weeks, and I think I already do after a few days.

We weren't so worried about you, and still aren't, having heard that you passed all tests with high honors and are now simply trying to think up a test you can't beat. You and I will outlive everybody, or at least you will, and I have a mighty good chance of lasting another twenty years unless I'm shot down like a rat in some alley by a plainclothesman. "Got him right through the Stevenson button," this fellow will say. I've got a couple of anonymous letters from one or two of the less cultured Eisenhower followers. One wants to know how much I got paid for my vote, and the other,

1. *New Yorker* contributor Frank Sullivan, who was in poor health. Thurber, now being treated for a thyroid condition, commiserated.

signed Mac Vigilante, says I'm a conceited and silly Trojan horse pro-Communist.

I want you to take it easy and get well fast, and I promise to do the same, and Helen sends us both her love and best wishes in this regard.

When I got home from New York yesterday, there was your note, but how the hospital knew where to reach me I'll never know, except that it's the most accurate hospital in the world.

Love and kisses, Frank, and be of good cheer.

As always,

JIM

Thurber and Donald Ogden Stewart, boyhood friends in Columbus, had an unexpected reunion at a London party.

◄◄►►

Stafford Hotel
London, England
August 1, 1958

Dear old boy:

What a wonderful evening that was, and there couldn't have been a better place or time for us two East Siders and graduates of Sullivant and Douglas schools to get together. As I recall it, through the smoke and gin, we ended up having been born only six minutes and a block-and-a-half apart.

I got a magnificent letter next day from our host,[1] who is really a wonderful man as well as musician, also a phone call from Hy Kraft,[2] and I want to see them again, as well as you and Ella,[3] when we get back from the country. We are going away for two weeks to finish the goddam Ross book — maybe Helen told you that she is writing a novel about me called *By Ross Possessed.* I usually take six to eight weeks to finish any piece — that is, when I'm at my so-called best — but I have darned near finished the five final chapters of the Ross book in six weeks here. It is easier to write in London than in New York. . . .

By the way, my small piece in *Punch* a couple of weeks ago dealt with the perils of typo and garble, and how meaning can be completely reversed. One example I used was "Don, give up the ship." I left out one that I'm using for *Holiday* in a piece *The New Yorker* rejected. It seems to me it would make a wonderful sign for the walls of S. Klein's and those other tough New York department stores that have framed copies of newspaper stories about shop-

---

1. Harmonica player Larry Adler.
2. A Hollywood scriptwriter.
3. Stewart's wife Ella, the widow of Lincoln Steffens.

lifters who have been arrested and punished: "God help those who help themselves." . . .

As ever,

J<small>IM</small>

The intensity of Thurber's interest in poetry and grammar is reflected in this letter to Lewis Gannett, literary critic of the New York Herald Tribune. *The Thurbers were Connecticut neighbors of Gannett and his wife Ruth.*

◄◄►►

West Cornwall,
Connecticut
June 25, 1956

Dear old boy:

You are completely right in that Fowler[1] says what you said he had said, *mutatis* a trifle *mutandis,* but at the risk of being hit with another smug, I say he is spinach in this particular case and I say the hell with him. The Fowlers were not often wrong, but some of their untenable positions have become notorious at the Grammarians' Club, of which I was once recording secretary. Fowler (we usually make one out of both) was wonderful chiefly because of his nonpurist and often antipurist scholarship, and because of his love of controversy and his amazing *OED* fund of examples. What nobody who has written on the subject seems to have said about Felicia's awkward line[2] is that its wrongness grows out of her lousiness as a poet and her awkwardness as a writer.

The lady was clearly trying to say, "The boy stood on the burning deck after everybody else had left," and in my time I have done more than fifteen variations of this, none of them fitting the metrical scheme with which she had gyved her small mental wrists. It seems to me the simplest way to say what she was trying to say is this sentence: "The boy stood on the burning deck whence all save him had fled."

What causes all the trouble is the fact that the clumsy lady comes up with "but he had fled," which is a fool-the-eye-and-ear because

1. Henry Watson Fowler, assisted by his brother Francis, compiled *A Dictionary of Modern English Usage.*

2. English poet Felicia Dorothea Hemans's preferred opening for "Casabianca": "The boy stood on the burning deck / Whence all but he had fled."

it diverts the mind from the prepositional "but he" to the conjunc-
tive "but he had."

If Fowler was right, then the lady meant to say: "The boy stood
on the burning deck whence all had fled, but he had not." I think
Felicia was a simple "except him" girl, but she got into trouble with
her unfortunate use of "whence." She may have been the worst
writer of English that ever lived. What mainly keeps the sentence
from being poetical, however, is her tone-deaf use of "stood." She
did almost everything to make the sentence one of the greatest ram-
shackles of our language.

I am surprised that Fowler was behind his time and Churchill's
in calling "it is me" a blunder. The last of the two brothers, writing
through a friend to thank me for my "Our Own Modern English
Usage" (circa 1930), particularly liked my holding out for the pres-
ervation of "whom," which many people, including Henry Morgan,
would like to eliminate. I had said that it was necessary for the
purpose of hauteur in such expressions as "Whom are you any-
ways?"

I have been planning a piece on personal pronouns and the death
of the accusative. Nobody says "I gave it to they," but "me" is
almost dead, and I have heard its dying screams from Bermuda to
Columbus: "He gave it to Janey and I." (We have to thank Hart,
Rodgers, and O'Hara for the lovely attack on this.) My cousin Earl
Fisher said to me in Columbus, "Louise and I gave it to he and she
last Christmas."

Last night on television a woman announcer said, "It is one of
the electrical machines that cools. . . ." Since "that" is sometimes
forced to do the work of "which," and "which" is said to have the
authority of "and it," then "one" would properly be the subject of
the sentence. In our wonderful and awkward language anything can
be argued, but the lady was wrong as hell is wrong. What it means
is: "Of the electrical machines that cool, it is one." I would have
loved to meet, or I would love to have met, the Fowlers — at least
we all stood firm against "I would have loved to have met."

The English deplore *The New Yorker*'s commaphilia and speak of
"The Century of the Comma Mag." They object especially to such
things as this: "In the living room, the argument continued after
dinner." This would be necessary only if "room the argument"

were a common expression. In "After dinner coffee was served on the terrace" we have a sentence to drive a *New Yorker* editor crazy. The English know that "moreover" and "furthermore" carry their own commas. Furthermore I don't care what Fowler says about that. Eight years ago I exchanged letters with a punctilious punctuator in England.

The legend that Ross put a comma in "I saw her but a moment" because of the danger that the reader might misconstrue the fourth word is not true. Love to you and she from Helen and I.

As ever,

J<small>IM</small>

◄◄◇►►

A BIRTHDAY POEM FOR LEWIS GANNETT, MARCH 10, 1951

Listen, my children, and don't try to scan it —
To the midlife ride of Lewis Gannett.
By the time he was ten he had taught himself
To review the books on his father's shelf.
"The House of Mirth" and "Beautiful Joe,"
The horrible tales of E. A. Poe,
Mr. Bulfinch's Fabulous Age
and "Riders of the Purple Sage,"
The wondrous exploits of magic Alice,
And old "Ben-Hur" by General Wallace,
Owen Meredith's sweet "Lucile,"
"The Rover Boys & Their Automobile,"
Stevenson's tale of pirates and rum,
"The Little Shepherd of Kingdom Come,"
"Five Little Peppers & How They Grew,"
And Henry James's "Turn of the Screw,"
Somebody's "Life of Daniel Boone,"
"The Crimson Sweater" and "Lorna Doone."
A few old books his Dad kept in hiding,
(Not "The Little Colonel's Knight Came Riding").
The good old books are dead and gone,
But Lewis Gannett still marches on,
Reading a thousand volumes a year,
Full of blood and sex and fear.
"I Married a Serb," "I Killed My Wife,"
"I Die by Inches," "I Wrecked My Life,"
"Our Disappearing Food Supply,"
"The Russian Conquest of the Sky,"
"The Jig Is Up," "The Moon Is Down,"
"The Case of the Stain on the Virgin's Gown,"
"No Place to Hide," "Man's Day is Done,"
"The End of Peace," & "Our Race is Run,"
"The Death of Love," "We Bring Laughter,"
"Our Youth Is Sick," & "There's No Hereafter."

Such a gory list as freezes
Every bloodstream save "Louise's."
And let us toast a man of stone
Who's not afraid to read alone,
While the rest of us, in our reading circle,
Stick to the works of Angela Thirkell.

◄◆►

West Cornwall,
Connecticut
December 3, 1958

Dear Lewis:

It was mighty thoughtful of you to send me that quote from dear old Sam Adams's letter.[1] It has cheered my day and week in this cheerless season. Helen and I were talking about, only yesterday, as we have done before, the special gift both you and Ruth have of doing things for people. It is not the commonest human virtue. I have just got a wintry letter from Andy White who, when he is in one of his self-bound phases, is the most selfful of men. Fortunately, it arrived in the same mail with a warm letter from Frank Sullivan, which was followed by your letter. Andy made it clear that he liked some of my book on Ross, but did not want the publishers to mention him as contributing to it, because it is a book he does not thoroughly approve of. He says he "faded from me" when I got to "sex and money." Worst of all, and least like him, he says that he doesn't think he's going to like "your chapter on editing," because he has heard of high explosions in the sky over 44th Street[2] recently. The assumption that I would let recent fights with current editors there influence my book on Ross angers the hell out of me. I wrote him that that sentence was the most un-White sentence he ever wrote. It is not, however and alas, unsubcommittee.

But blessings on the Gannetts and Frank Sullivan and the soul of Sam Adams. Merry Christmas.

As always,

Jim

1. Samuel Hopkins Adams, the novelist.
2. Site of *The New Yorker*.

◄◄►►

West Cornwall,
Connecticut
December 18, 1958

Dear Kenneth:[1]

I was not at *The New Yorker* to roll out the red carpet for you for three reasons: chance, an overactive thyroid, and the feeling that you deserved the right to arrive and get settled in the traditional *New Yorker* manner. The tradition is, on the surface, cold, careless and inhospitable, but we all had to go through it, from me to Edmund Wilson, and I didn't want you to miss the strange experience.

I told Shawn that I knew and liked the Tynans and that I was tremendously happy that the magazine had the good sense to take you on after Gibbs went away into the undiscover'd country from whose bourn no traveler returns, except maybe Archibald MacLeish. I don't have to tell anybody who can read that you have brought a new and special brilliance, style, wit, and learning to the theatre page. What I have been afraid of, from the start, was that you would be worn down by some of the goddam stupidities, quibblings, and criticisms of a group of writers scarcely notable for learning, vocabulary, allusions, and the like. Just bare your teeth if they drive you nuts, which they will try to do, unintentionally, of course. . . .

I have waited until now to tell you about the final paragraph of what must have been the last letter Wolcott Gibbs ever wrote. It reached me in London about two weeks before he died. In the last paragraph he told me he intended to come to *The New Yorker* once a week this winter to defend his final corrected proofs against the inroads, and fumblings, of editors and punctuators intent on changing "my punctuation and my little jokes so that they would be clear to my cleaning woman." The present-day editors, caught somewhere between *The New Yorker*'s original naive anti-intellectualism and a curious oversimplified pretentiousness all their own, now and then send me, and most of the rest of us, into screaming orbit. . . .

---

1. Kenneth Tynan, the recently recruited drama critic from England.

May you stay away from the sobbing miseries, snarl the fumble-
minded sons-of-butchers into their proper place, and keep on writing that sound and beautiful and exciting stuff. Nothing has
pleased me more than your being on *The New Yorker.* Helen and I
look forward to seeing you and Miss Gorce sometime next month
when we get to New York again. Meanwhile, Merry Christmas and
God bless all Tynans.

As always,

J<small>IM</small>

Joel Sayre and his wife Gertrude were friends of Thurber's from Colum-
bus who had a daughter, Nora, about the same age as Rosemary. Time
wished to get an accurate cover story on Thurber but assigned it to an
inexperienced reporter who had never heard of the humorist, and the
result was a mess. Joe Sayre, who had worked on The New Yorker,
was then commissioned to do a new article. Thurber supplied him with
material, especially about a series he was writing at the time, which
became The Thurber Album.

◄◄►►

West Cornwall,
Connecticut
December 12, 1950

Dear Joe:

. . . I am about halfway through the piece on my mother for the
series. It has taken me six months off and on — the whole thing
started three years ago, and I have worked on it longer than any
other project, having rewritten all the stories in proof. There will
also be a piece on two of my Ohio State professors, Joe Taylor and
Joe Denney, and this is shaping up fine, thanks to marvelous help
given me by Getz,[1] who actually wrote to twelve friends of the men
for me. Then there will be a piece on seven or eight assorted characters in my mother's family, all of them too fantastic to be believed, including Jake Fisher, of the airship, old Mary Griffin, Doc
Beall, who said "poppycock!" about all medical ideas except his
own, was opposed to bathing on the ground that it opened the
pores to disease, and believed in getting his bare feet on the ground
even when it was covered with snow. He wore a top hat, cutaway,
and black bow tie, and his white hair stood straight up because he
was buried alive during a plague, he said. I think this book will
run to fifty thousand words, and I will probably bring it out next
fall illustrated with some wonderful old family photographs my
mother has. The pieces will run in *The New Yorker* about every

1. Lester Getzloe of the O.S.U. journalism department.

three weeks, and the boys around here seem to think it is one of my best things and that the piece on Mrs. Albright[2] may be my best one. I have lived with this series — you know how that goes — and they arbitrarily started it on me, knowing that I would rewrite it in proof the rest of my life.

If you have any questions, old boy, pass them on to me. The material you had to look through must have astounded you. Incidentally, I had lunch with T. S. Eliot the other day and Helen and I were crazy about him. We went to Robert's,[3] had two martinis, then scrambled eggs and bacon, after which he wanted chocolate ice cream, and we all had that. He had been up pretty late at a party and, I think, was glad we didn't insist on fancy food with sauce and wine, which he says he can't drink at noon. *Time* tried to find out what cigarette he smokes but couldn't. It turns out he smokes Kools. . . .

Love and kisses,

As ever,

JIM

2. "Aunt Margery" Albright, the nursemaid who tended Thurber during his boyhood.
3. A French restaurant.

◂◆▸

West Cornwall,
Connecticut
December 13, 1950

Dear Joe:

Pursuant to yesterday's communique, I got a brief note from Ross splitting an infinitive as follows: "Tell Sayre to damn well and soon return those proofs." . . .

Funny thing about reviews of *The 13 Clocks*. I had predicted Orville Prescott's[1] would be bad and that I would get about 80 percent good and this has been so. The *Hartford Times* finds the story is "meaningless," apparently because it is innocent of satire or moral. What is the meaning of "Cinderella?" I think it must be that if you can ride in a pumpkin without catching pneumonia you are lucky. Or what good does it do to have the smallest foot in the world if you can't hitch white mice. I wrote the story because I had fun and was hiding. . . .

Look out for those curve balls.

As ever,

JIM

1. In the *New York Times*.

◄ ◄ ► ►

West Cornwall,
Connecticut
December 22, 1950

Dear Joe:

   . . . If you are doing the *Time* piece you might want to know that people write me about my eye from all parts of the world. Americans suggest watching jumping beans, rubbing my spine, injecting lemon juice, applying hot flatirons to the temple, and using the urine of virgins. A man in Birmingham, England, sent me black paper and an aluminum pencil, and I just got a letter from a doctor named Van Der Merwe suggesting tubercle endotoxoid injections. Bruce's material was sent to you. *Time* mucked up the eye story in the Darrah piece.

   Helen and Rosie and I send you Christmas greetings again and our love.

As always,

JIM

◄◄►►

West Cornwall,
Connecticut
December 22, 1950

Dear Joe:

A little crotch-kicking is a good thing, if done in anger. I can't stand guys who are merely piqued by the unforgivable. . . . Good deportment is a minor virtue in a man, but God's own comfort to his friends. . . .

. . . *The White Deer* has been the basis of sermons and Christmas readings in one or two Episcopalian churches, and I was astonished to find I had done in the last chapter a modern restatement of the Atonement beginning "What you have been you now no longer are."

One of the things I most resent is the idiotic use of the word "genius" for me, and when it came up on Mary Margaret McBride's program the other day I said I was a reporter without enough genius to get off newspapers and make more than forty a week until I was thirty-two. Anybody with the slightest critical ability knows that a genius would not have to slave over his prose so long, or over his drawings so little. The geniuses are O'Hara and Sally Benson and Peter Blume and Hendrik van Loon. First drafts of my pieces sound twelve years old and only get going on the fourth rewrite. I have never cut off an ear or stuck my hand in a fire. . . .

The proof of humor is the ability to put one's self on awkward public record, just as the proof of wit is to do that to others; and while we are going in for profound definitions, the proof of solicitude is not avoidance, and the maddest I get is at people who avoid discussing my eye on the ridiculous ground that it would embarrass me. . . . There is too much talk about the courage or nobility of the afflicted, since I know damn well that the challenge is far greater than the handicap. Remember that one-legged newsboy in Columbus who went on the vaudeville stage, and look at the average paraplegic absorbed in learning skills and tricks. I saw an armless woman in a movie short wrapping bundles with her feet, and hav-

Opportunity

ing more fun than you and I have with our hands. Furthermore, I
have been spared the sight of television. . . .

More later, and once again love and kisses and a Merry Christmas.

As ever,

JIM

◄◄►►

Waterville Inn
Paget East, Bermuda
June 1, 1954

Dear Joe:

. . . We are deeply concerned to hear about Gertrude's coming operations, in a letter that Janie received from Ann Allen[1] the other day. My God, hasn't that girl had enough to endure! Tell her we keep thinking about her all the time and can certainly understand that she would want to get that hip condition straightened out, but she has had more than her share of hospitals.

We see a lot of the Williamses, that great big lovely and healthy family, and they all send their love and best wishes to Gertrude and you. It has been almost twenty-two years since you were at "Shorelee" and it doesn't seem a day over seventeen.

It's been wonderful here without television and with the McCarthy news pushed over onto page 4. You can spend three hours at a cocktail party and never hear him mentioned. I wait for the moment when he will make a slip of the tongue and call Eisenhower "Hindenburg."

We met Admiral Carney[2] at the Naval Operations Base and thought he was a fine man. Our consul general here is a Columbus man named Streeper,[3] about two years younger than me. Our naval installation is bigger than ever and seems to be made up largely of southern Confederates. They are wonderful singers at a party, taking on everything from "Red River Valley" to "It was sad when the great ship went down. . . ." They come from the Carolinas and from Texas and one of them showed up at midnight dressed in a Confederate general's uniform. They are clearly all ready to go again as soon as South Carolina's patience gives out. . . .

Love and kisses to Gertrude and you from us both.

As always,

JIM

1. Widow of Hervey Allen.
2. Robert Bostwick Carney.
3. Robert B. Streeper.

◄◄◊►

Hôtel Continental
Paris, France
August 27, 1955

Dearest Gertrude:

. . . We have met a dozen American girls of the generation of
Nora and Rosie, who have been over here for a year or longer, and
it is remarkable and cheering to see how they have all developed
on their own. I have been thinking of writing a piece about the
American girl in France and England, based on this element of the
development of self-assurance and accomplishment on their own.
They seem to spring into a kind of bloom when they get out from
under American pressures and have to fend for themselves, which
they do extremely well. None of them is adjusted better than Nora,
and I think you and Joe should be proud of her and encourage her
to stay on for another year or so. In my Paris years, during the
twenties, there were few American girls here and a great many
men, but now the situation is reversed.

Nora has shown great skill and application in the research she
has done for me,[1] and you need have no fears or worries about her
at all, for she certainly knows how to take care of herself. I hope
that my granddaughter can someday have two years on her own in
Europe, after my delighted observation of the girls of Rosie's and
Nora's age.

They will be all the better for it when they get back to America.
Nora, of course, has made a great many friends and contacts, and I
knew, when I first saw her in London, that her European phase was
a good one. I now see that my own first two years in Paris, after the
First War, meant a lot to my later adjustment in New York. There
was a large family in Columbus and too little chance for the practice
of self-reliance. Our American way of life is so terribly intramural,
whereas over here the children are more often on their own, just as
husbands and wives usually spend a part of each summer apart.
American mothers need not worry about their daughters and

---

1. Thurber hired her to help research his pieces on the Loch Ness monster.

should take heed of the story of Liz Gude, who stayed at a pension here with another girl her age. The woman who runs the pension sent her son of the same age to visit relations in the country, because French mothers are just as alarmed about American girls as mothers back home are about the French boys! . . .

As ever,

JIM

MR. THURBER REGRETS

No writer has ever declined so many time-consuming requests with such grace.

◄◄►►

West Cornwall,
Connecticut
March 23, 1950

Mr. John C. Spence
Director of Public Relations
Fraternity Affairs Office
Columbus, Ohio

Dear Mr. Spence:

I'm afraid I can't go along with your idea that a man's success, whatever it may be, is due to his having belonged to a fraternity in college. Your letter gives me the uncomfortable feeling that you are setting the fraternity man against the non-fraternity man in a rather cloudy and panicky effort to shield fraternities from public criticism, much of which is richly deserved. I know of no fraternity man who is at present doing more for his country than Herbert Hoover, a non-fraternity graduate of Stanford.

There is always a kind of candied incandescence when fraternity people talk about the importance of fraternities, and this betrays an entirely false set of values. Fraternities are extremely private organizations and, by their nature, subject to no realistic relationship to the general public. I think that a program like yours would have value only if both sides of the question were squarely presented. As it is, you seem to be in a great and puzzling hurry to protect fraternities from something by the utterly false procedure of associating success with fraternities. I cannot take part in such a curious undertaking.

Sincerely yours,

JAMES THURBER

After-Dinner Music: Thurber and Sandburg

◄◄►►

West Cornwall,
Connecticut
January 30, 1951

Miss Margaret H. Ligon, Librarian
Pack Memorial Public Library
Asheville, North Carolina

Dear Miss Ligon:

Nobody ever gives me time to get things done, and such a project as yours can't be batted off. I wouldn't want to start writing in January something about Carl Sandburg to be finished in January. He may seem as easy to describe as a face carved on a mountain, but there are vast and complex reaches between the cat feet of the "Fog" and "Remembrance Rock." I like to think of him informally, without putting on my stiff Sunday critical shirt and shoes. He was up here not too long ago, playing his guitar and singing, sometimes with me, late into the night, although it seemed early. I was proud to have taught him a new verse about Casey Jones, who went through Toledo on an open switch. He is an American institution, not easy to describe within the limits of January. Let the glib boys do that, and give him my love and fond wishes that he will go on forever.

Best wishes for your show.

Sincerely yours,

JAMES THURBER

◄◄►►

West Cornwall,
Connecticut
March 17, 1958

Messrs. Dave Kussow and Tom Chopin
De Pere, Wisconsin

Dear Boys:

You can tell where I get my ideas from the things I write, and then you will know as much about it as I do. To write about people you have to know people, to write about bloodhounds you have to know bloodhounds, to write about the Loch Ness monster you have to find out about it. I write because I have to write and it's a good thing a writer gets paid. If I juggled because I have to juggle I couldn't live. You will have to ask my readers why they read what I write. I hope they read it because it has something to say. You can also say that writers could get more written if they didn't have to answer so many questions about why they write.

Best wishes.

Sincerely yours,

JAMES THURBER

The editor of Omnibook *had proposed publishing a condensation of* The Thurber Album.

➤◄◆►◄

West Cornwall,
Connecticut
June 23, 1952

Mr. M. M. Geffen
Omnibook
New York City, New York

Dear Mr. Geffen:
   I'm sorry you had to go to all that trouble, but you showed me clearly what you have in mind so that I can deal with it reasonably. Too many grace notes and too much of my heart go out in the cutting. I could not permit a word of Mrs. Albright to be changed, for just one point. I appreciate *Omnibook*'s vast problem, which is to convince itself that there are too many lines in a sonnet and too many stars and one unnecessary color in the flag. It is a hell of a job you have, and I send you my sympathy together with the shaking of a disapproving finger. There are men who can be cut profitably, like Thomas Wolfe, maybe. Fitzgerald wrote him once, "You are a putter in and I am a taker out." I must have taken out a hundred thousand words, but this old-fashioned sofa can't lose any more stuffing.
   I winked at your lovely sister in a postscript once, but I have never had the good luck to meet any Geffens. Maybe my luck will change. I hope so.

Sincerely yours,

JAMES THURBER

◄◆►

West Cornwall,
Connecticut
July 8, 1949

Miss Ada Laura Fonda Snell
Mount Holyoke College
South Hadley, Massachusetts

Dear Miss Snell:

. . . Fifteen years ago and more, I sometimes talked briefly to English classes at Ohio State, on which frightening occasions my nervousness made the class nervous, setting up a nervous cycle. We were both glad when it was over. Since 1940, when I lost the ability to read and to get around by myself, I have had to abandon what one friend called my public apparitions. . . .

I was pleased and honored, so was Helen, to receive your invitation, and I am distressed that I have to decline, since I love Mount Holyoke. The idea of addressing the flower of American womanhood would terrify me even if I could see. I am like the tough American soldier, loose in no-man's-land during the First War, who had invaded a dozen enemy trenches with a lone companion, capturing a hundred Germans, and who suddenly came upon a dark, mysterious, and deep hole in the ground. He peered into it cautiously. "You goin' down there, Mac?" asked his friend. Mac looked at the hole again. "I wouldn't go down there," he said, "if they was Fig Newtons down there."

Your name is like a waving flag and should never be furled in abbreviation. Helen joins me in thanking you for your invitation, and we send you our joint regrets. I hope that I will have the pleasure someday of meeting you.

Cordially yours,

JAMES THURBER

◄◄◆►

West Cornwall,
Connecticut
August 3, 1949

Miss M. J. Call
Miss E. Gillespie
New Orleans, Louisiana

Dear ladies:

Harold Ross, a timid man who is easily terrified, sent your letter on to me and I have been picking it up and putting it down. Nobody has been interested in my looks for a long time, including myself. I don't have any pictures around, and I haven't had any taken for many years, except by newspaper photographers and the like. Maybe a couple will turn up one of these days, and so I will keep your letter on file in a folder all by itself. Ross has a far more interesting face and there ought to be photographs of him in your city, since he worked on a newspaper there years ago. I am delighted, of course, that two southern belles know their way around in my books and would like to know what kind of man acts that way. Everybody else is writing for pictures of Montgomery Clift.

Best wishes to you both,

Sincerely yours,

JAMES THURBER

►◄◊►►

Williamsburg Inn
Williamsburg,
Virginia
March 21, 1953

Mr. Richard Maney
New York City, New York

Dear Dick:

Why do so many people who can't write plays write plays? This ought to be easy for you. I read the first scene of *Take a Giant Step* and that was enough. I regret to say I had hoped our hero would get his block knocked off, and I was disappointed when he was suspended for only a week after attacking Smith, insulting his teacher, and smoking a cigar. People never learn that there is 1,000 miles of desert between a good cause and a good play. Few people can cross it alive.

Helen, who has always been crazy about you, joins me in love and kisses.

As ever,

JIM

◄◄◆►►

West Cornwall,
Connecticut
November 23, 1955

Mr. Harrison Kinney
McCall's
New York City, New York

Dear Harrison:

All that *McCall's* and I have in common is you. A magazine that calls itself "the magazine of togetherness" finds me in favor of aparture from it. I came back from Europe with a dozen commitments, I'm blind as a bat, and will be sixty-one next month. As the fellow said, "Sunset and evening star, and no *McCall's* for me."

Helen joins me in a Merry Christmas to you and the magazine of togetherness.

As ever,

J*IM*

►◄►►

West Cornwall,
Connecticut
July 12, 1957

Mr. Bill Grauer
Bill Grauer Productions
New York City, New York

Dear Mr. Grauer:
   I'll have to wait, in any case, until the fall, because of work, dead-
lines, bad allergy and throat, summer depression, and a sworn intention to preserve this old house for my writing only, and not for
television, radio, recordings, ballet, pantomime or my own production of *Tobacco Road* with me as Jeeter Lester.

Cordially yours,

JAMES THURBER

◄◇►

West Cornwall,
Connecticut
January 4, 1958

Mr. Robert Leifert
New York City, New York

Dear Robert:

Since a hundred schoolchildren a year write me letters like yours — some writers get a thousand — the problem of what to do about such classroom "projects" has become a serious one for all of us. If a writer answered all of you he would get nothing else done. When I was a baby goat I had to do my own research on projects, and I enjoyed doing it. I never wrote an author for his autograph or photograph in my life. Photographs are for movie actors to send to girls. Tell your teacher I said so, and please send me her name. . . .

One of the things that discourage us writers is the fact that 90 percent of you children write wholly, or partly, illiterate letters, carelessly typed. You yourself write "clarr" for "class" and that's a honey, Robert, since *s* is next to *a,* and *r* is on the line above. Most schoolchildren in America would do a dedication like the following (please find the mistakes in it and write me about them):

> *To Miss Effa G. Burns*
> *Without who's help*
> *this book could never*
> *of been finished it,*
> *is dedicated with*
> *gartitude by it's*
> *arthur.*

Show that to your teacher and tell her to show it to her principal, and see if they can find the mistakes. . . .

Just yesterday a letter came in from a girl your age in South Carolina asking for biographical material and photograph. That is not the kind of education they have in Russia, we are told, because it's too much like a hobby or waste of time. What do you and your classmates want to be when you grow up — collectors? Then who is going to help keep the United States ahead of Russia in science, engineering, and the arts?

Please answer this letter. If you don't I'll write to another pupil.

Sincerely yours,

JAMES THURBER

◄◄◆►►

West Cornwall,
Connecticut
July 1, 1960

Mrs. Anne Hodge
Ginn & Company
Dallas, Texas

Dear Mrs. Hodge:

All my best wishes for a quick recovery go to Ben Wheeler, but I have no intention of aiding and abetting the circulation of that drawing. Done nearly thirty years ago for Harold Ross, it shows a man with an enormous thing, as you women call it, saying, "Hello, folks" to popeyed nude women and scowling little nude men. Ross had a hundred copies made and sent to friends of his, including Mencken and Groucho Marx, without my knowing about it. Further copies are now circulated in smoking cars and bars by leering guys. Hallelujah, sister, let us turn our minds to something more rewarding.

Cordially yours,

JAMES THURBER

◄◄►►

West Cornwall,
Connecticut
July 31, 1959

Mr. Robert Emmett Ginna
Horizon
New York City, New York

Dear Mr. Ginna:

Having been photographed and interviewed fifty times in fourteen months, I have lost weight, sleep badly, and hate photographers, especially the artistic ones who take 200 shots of their subjects at one sitting. I do not call this art, but some kind of
compulsion, like opening oysters in the hope of finding a pearl in
one of them. There are now eleven million photographs of me in
this country and abroad, taken by Cartier-Bresson, Cecil Beaton,
Avedon, Douglas Glass, Halsman, and on and on. I know when I
have had enough.

I like *Horizon* and think your project is wonderful, but I want to
survive this year.

Cordially yours,

JAMES THURBER

◄◄◊►►

West Cornwall,
Connecticut
August 15, 1959

Mr. Judson Irish
Ogilvy, Benson & Mather
New York City, New York

Dear Mr. Irish:

I was startled to learn that the A.A.A.A.,[1] with which I have always been on dog-and-cat terms, should so sincerely and eloquently ask me to perform as outlined in your letter. If I were younger and could see anything at all I would appear or let someone make a film and recording, but I have simply had to give up all such outside shenanigans. Since June of 1959 I have been interviewed and photographed some thirty times — newspaper, magazine, radio, television — in London and Paris and New York, and I have had to wave the white flag and hide. My wife and doctor and Mother Nature have all put their foot down. I am today answering seven letters from people who want to come up and take only a little bit of my time. Youngsters now bring babble boxes for me to talk into, as we sink further and further into the new Oral Culture. The written word will soon disappear and we'll no longer be able to read good prose like we used to could. This prospect does not gentle my thoughts or tranquil me toward the future.

Thanks anyway and I hope those creative spirits learn how to get through to the people the literate way.

Sincerely yours,

JAMES THURBER

1. American Association of Advertising Agencies.

►◄◊►

Stafford Hotel
London, England
February 23, 1961

Robert Reilly
Schenectady, New York

Dear Robert:

I always tell everybody who asks, "If you are a writer you write."

O. Henry once said, "The only rule for writing short stories is that there is no rule." You should take all kinds of courses in high school and college, because a general education is the best foundation for a writing career.

It is also important to read good books and nobody should try to be a writer until he reaches twenty-four years of age. I didn't get started on *The New Yorker* until I was thirty-two, and the first of my twenty-seven books came out when I was thirty-five.

Good luck.

Sincerely yours,

JAMES THURBER

-◄-◇-►-

West Cornwall,
Connecticut
July 5, 1961

Miss Marianna Brown
Cincinnati, Ohio

Dear Marianna Brown:

 The past is an old armchair in the attic, the present an ominous
ticking sound, and the future anybody's guess. It was fun back
there with the Rover Boys, the Little Colonel, Pollyanna, and Peg-
o'-my-Heart, but we don't want to be caught in the past while the
Russians are shaking hands with the Martians. Let us then be up
and doing.

Sincerely yours,

JAMES THURBER

At: The Stafford Hotel,
        St. James's Place,
            London, S.W.1.

2nd May 1961.

Mr. Norman A. Kurland,
Chase C-42,
Harvard Business School,
Boston 63, MASS.
U.S.A.

Dear Mr. Kurland,

         I had to give up public appearances when I

became a hundred and went blind nearly twenty years ago, and,

besides, I am now in Europe and in the Fall expect to be in

Jeopardy.

         Thanks anyway, and all best wishes,

                    Sincerely yours,

                    [signature]

            JAMES THURBER.

"DEAR TED
AND
CHARLIE"

In January 1957 Edward Weeks, editor of The Atlantic Monthly, *and Charles W. Morton, his associate editor, who had once been on the staff of* The New Yorker, *wrote to Thurber urging him to prepare a portrait of Harold Ross for* The Atlantic's *centennial issue in November. Thurber at first declined, although he had actually started such a project years earlier. In July he told Morton he would do it and in September warned that there was too much material for a single piece.*

Thurber went on to write the most widely read serial in The Atlantic's *history — ten articles that formed the substance of his book* The Years with Ross.

◄◄◆►►

West Cornwall,
Connecticut
January 18, 1957

Dear Mr. Morton:

I have written fifteen thousand letters in the past ten years and I don't know what happened to your old letter about Ross. I write a

hundred editors, publishers, agents, professors, sick people, crazy people, children, and old ladies every six weeks. Where did *The Atlantic* get this silly notion? You have been circling around me like the Indians around Custer. People often call me on the phone about things, from Washington to Delhi, or from bars in St. Louis or San Diego, and most of them I never heard of.

I have not finished twenty thousand words about Ross, but merely roughed them out. I rewrite everything from ten to twenty-five times. I don't know that I want it published in any magazine. Many have been after it, including *Harper's* and *Esquire*. I turned down *Esquire* flat. . . . I appreciate your interest in Ross and in my piece, but think you're pretty funny pussyfooting and tiptoeing around little old me as if I were Count Keyserling[1] or someone. My highest regard to Mr. Weeks and you, and a happy life.

Cordially yours,

THURBER

1. Social philosopher Hermann Alexander Keyserling, author of *America Set Free*.

✦

FROM CHARLES W. MORTON

Boston,
Massachusetts
August 5, 1957

Dear Jim:

The best thing about pursuing you for *Atlantic* material is the predictability of the result: It's bound to be wonderful. So, it was with certitude that I started to read your first installment this morning. It seems to me the perfect article to begin a series, and it transmits successfully the whole range of Ross's personality. I should have despaired myself of trying to describe on paper his constant dream of finding the super-editor-administrator, but you have caught it to the least nuance. I believe Ted Weeks has expressed to your wife his profound satisfaction in the manuscript, and I was most pleased to learn that we had arrived at proper terms. I hope there will be four, or more than four, instead of three, but in either case we are looking ahead excitedly to having the series in print. . . .

As ever yours,

CHARLIE

►◄◄►►

West Cornwall,
Connecticut
August 6, 1957

Dear Charlie:

The Years with Ross

That title came to me last night while talking with my guardian angel, and Helen and I think it is right. My story takes in more than mere working with Ross. I am working on him now and hard. I'm glad you liked the first piece. They get better.

Cordially,

Jim

◄◄◆►►

West Cornwall,
Connecticut
February 11, 1958

Dear Charlie:

I got Part VI down to almost eighteen pages, ahead of tight schedule, and you will have it by now. . . .

The rest of the series shapes up like this, so far as I can tell now: Part VII, More Miracle Men; Part VIII, Sex and Other Hell in the Office, which should be the funniest piece; Part IX, Ross Outside the Office, as fisherman, host, and guest, and above all things, wag. This takes in his incredible friendship with Woollcott, full of gags, cruel and otherwise. Part X will probably deal with some outstanding editorial crises and systems, including Gibbs's nineteen (I think) brief and amusing rules for editing the magazine, and the final part will be concerned with winding it up, including an attempt years ago to oust [Ross], and my experience with him in London and Paris, and his final months. . . .

Since I have dictated or written four times as much as has got into print or reached you, my wife and secretary are not sure whether I actually incorporated in some earlier piece in *The Atlantic* the incident of "The Mistakes Made by J. Thurber" and the "firing of the man responsible and of Miss so-and-so." I wrote that three different times in earlier drafts, but feel sure it didn't reach print. The only other things for your checkers to look for are whether I have mentioned "My Life on a Limb" and the exact wording of the brief quote from James Branch Cabell. It appears on a flyleaf of one of his novels which I read decades ago, probably one of these: *The High Place, Something about Eve,* or *The Cords of Vanity.*

Best wishes, and ring me up when ready, Gridley.

JIM

P.S. Here's a quote from a letter to me written by Bernard Hollowood, editor of *Punch:* "May I say that everyone at *Punch* is reading your Ross stuff with enormous interest and enjoyment: we just can't get the damn *Atlantic* fast enough."

When he had completed ten chapters of The Years with Ross, *Thurber commissioned thirteen short pieces by former contributors to* The New Yorker, *which he paid for and intended to include as "End Papers." With the exception of "Ross at the Wheel" by E. B. White, they lacked the sparkle and quality of what Thurber had written and they did not impress the judges of the Book-of-the-Month Club, one of whom, John Mason Brown, termed the book "disorganized." Those were fighting words.*

◄◆►

FROM HELEN THURBER

Hôtel Continental
Paris, France
October 19, 1958

Dear Ted and Charlie:

Your letters were quite a blow to us, after the horribly hard summer we had and the trip really ruined. I blame myself primarily, for when I made the plans last winter, I expected the book to be done, as did we all, and finally, I had to get away or go crazy. I felt that if I lived in our house one more week with both Ross and Thurber, something would crack — probably me — and a change of locale would be good. I was wrong, I see now. For if we had been in closer touch, so much time and labor wouldn't have been wasted, for we would have had your reactions as we went along. I really hit the ceiling the day we got your letters, and Jim spent the day calming me down. Then, when I was in a calmer, what-the-hell mood, he reread the letters and blew up (mostly, I'm afraid, at your "Ross would not have allowed this," which I think was a little below the belt and not quite accurate under the circumstances).

What I regret most is that, since you had such severe reservations about the order of chapters (our order was hurried and entirely tentative) and about the End Papers and, for all we can tell, about the six new chapters Jim spent his holiday on, you didn't let us know before you submitted the book. We are not entirely unreasonable,

and certainly would have agreed to changes, omissions, and a reor-
dering of the chapters. I was against the End Papers from the very
beginning, before I read them and saw how uneven they were. My
objection, and I think it is the soundest one, is that after the warm
and moving last chapter about Ross's death, they were a terrible
anticlimax. Even if they had all been good, I still feel that way. You,
Charlie, reacted very lukewarmly to the idea of End Papers, but
hedged on it, as did I, and again I blame myself for this. . . .

Affectionately,

HELEN

►◄◊►►

Hôtel Continental
Paris, France
October 20, 1958

Dear Ted and Charlie:

All the End Papers will have to come out, and you surely must understand why. I cannot play favorites with old friends of mine on *The New Yorker*. I have paid them $3,000, which under no circumstances would I take back. I am devoted to only one thing now, to get this book off my mind and soul forever, with as little cost in anguish, broken friendship and money as possible.

White's "Ross at the Wheel" must go into the body of the book, in "Ross, Not Tobogganing."[1] I will be glad to cut other stuff in that piece, and end with the White piece.

The book, as it was, was simply not too long for its interest, and I am afraid I can't go along with a great deal you have to say about that. I will eliminate the End Papers for only one consideration: I realize that I strut through the major part of the book in full dress uniform, and let the other boys huddle in the back room in one-piece bathing suits. Liebling and the others can sell their pieces wherever they want to.

I consider the major mistake was that you submitted the book to the book club too hastily, and in disorganized manuscript form. I am making no changes whatever because of that club's criticisms. Eighteen years ago, one of their judges dismissed *The Male Animal* with a curt salute and the word "homespun." Another has recently called some of my best writing "finicky." Let's not mention any of them again.

The one thing that angers me most is the word "disorganized," and your statement that I cannot jump from 1927 to 1948, and back again. This is precisely what I set out to do, exactly the way I describe my purpose in Chapter I; and to Gibbs and other critics, it is precisely the effect, exactly the kind of unity this book should have. If I were a conformist, I would never have drawn any drawings, or

1. Retitled "Who Was Harold, What Was He?" in the book.

written much of anything else. This is not a formal biography, it says in the book, but will leap from point to point. I suggest you go back and read that. Gibbs writes in the foreword of his book, "It should always serve as a model for reminiscences of this sort." The dozens of letters you and I have received prove that it is, as one man put it, "a new and interesting form of biography."

I will permit the changes you suggest, and probably others, but I will not permit a rigid and sorry "organization" of the chapters in order to achieve the very thing I was trying to get away from.

Now that I have largely lost interest in this cumbersome venture, I will even take out most of the chapters done abroad, but certain things must stay in the book. If only the chapters used in *The Atlantic* are published in the book, I will really raise hell.

We must get this book over with within a short time after we come back to New York. I suggest that you indicate all your suggested cuts and stuff on one copy of the book, and that we go over it as quickly as possible in New York. Some of the Foreword will have to be eliminated now.

I am now engaged in writing one or two pieces of fiction, and intend to devote the rest of my life to plays and fiction. I shall certainly never take on a real person again, living or dead, saint or sinner. . . .

As ever,

Jim

◄◄►►

Hôtel Continental
Paris, France
October 24, 1958

Dear Ted:

I am enclosing a copy of a letter to Andy White, and a copy of the new beginning for my Foreword. They are self-explanatory. I insist that the Foreword should now begin as it does in the enclosure. I had to battle with *The New Yorker* about my unity of effect from 1927 onward, but the critics of my books have invariably agreed with me and not with the jumpy editors and publishers I have had to deal with. I respect and even admire their nervous dedication, but I cannot let it affect my work too seriously. I strongly urge you not to get too panicky about organization. *My Life and Hard Times*, in English, is now used in the schools of France with a foreword and comments by Jean Claire Auffrey. I looked at this book the other day, and it speaks of my "skilful disorganization." This was also pointed out twenty-five years ago by no less a critic than David Garnett, who clearly perceived the nature of my method, and had something like this to say in his review in a London journal: "The uninitiated reader may jump to the hasty conclusion that this book was dashed off between teatime and dinner, but it has clearly been put together with loving care, and I suggest that the operation must have required at least one year." Mr. Garnett was exactly right.

I am afraid that the final decision on the length of the book and the order of the chapters must be made by the man who put them together, the only man in the world who knows how they should go. I can say this with confidence now that I have realized where I did make my mistakes. I hope you and Charlie also realized where you made yours.

My affection and admiration for both of you remains as firm as ever. I have been through thirty years of this kind of thing, and my own firmness is pretty strong.

As ever,

J*IM*

◄◄◆►

West Cornwall,
Connecticut
November 25, 1958

Dear Charlie:

I have slenderized and shaped the new chapters, rewriting and cutting out to make them conform to the others. Further cuts, if needed, can be made on proofs. I don't think there is much more to be done.

We will read the proofs, from beginning to end, carefully, and so should somebody up there. Publishers and typists are notorious for ruinous typos — in the typing of these six pieces there are such things as "us" for "up" and "quotas" for "quotes." *Harper's* let sixty-seven such mistakes get into Janet Flanner's last book. Such sloppiness can cook the book. A blind man's repetitions of incidents must be watched for. I dream of such crap as "Journey's End in Livers Meeting" and "The Custard Pies of Frederick Stand." . . .

The Years with Ross is now a great big valentine, but what the hell, *toujours gai.* Let somebody else write *The Tears with Ross.*

Love from us both. I appreciate and admire the way you have gone through this ordeal with an aging and yelling writer.

As ever,

JIM

P.S. I have put you back in the Foreword, as you will see, and I cut out all the snarling.

The Years with Ross, *when revised, was accepted as an alternate se-lection by the Book-of-the-Month Club. This letter from Frank Sullivan to Morton speaks for the many old-timers who relished the book, as does the letter that follows it, from Stanley Walker, one of the earliest of the many managing editors of* The New Yorker.

◄◄►►

FROM FRANK SULLIVAN

Saratoga Springs,
New York
October 19, 1957

Dear Charlie:

A thousand thanks for sending me that proof of Jim's first install-ment on Ross. It is just as grand as I knew it would be and makes me surer than ever that I was right about Jim being the man to do the series. I had a letter from Jim asking me about any memories I had of Ross, and indeed I had and have many. I sent him all I could remember, and I sent him also all the letters from Ross to me that I could uncover. They are marvelous. One that I doubt if *The Atlantic* or any other magazine could print was a note that Ross sent with a proof he was returning to me. In it he said something like "Don't hesitate to complain if you think I've f——d up this piece" (only Ross didn't use any dashes) — then that gave him an idea, and he went on something like this: "And by the way, I wish you and O'Hara would stop writing letters to me full of words like (and he named a few of the four-letters) because they are apt to be read by pure young girls around this office, and I don't want them cor-rupted."

Jim's series is going to be great.

Yours,

FRANK

◄◄►►

FROM STANLEY WALKER

Lampasas, Texas
February 18, 1958

Dear Mr. Morton:

Well, I'd have hired you if it had been possible.[1] It's a wonder we didn't all starve to death in that remote time. Thanks for copies of *The Atlantic*. Out here in the hills we have a subscription arrangement with three or four literate friends, and we usually do pretty well, but the deal on *The Atlantic* went wrong somewhere. As Ross would say, the goddam system broke down.

The Thurber articles on Ross are as nearly perfect as such a job could be. He is the only man able to do full justice to that remarkable, exasperating, many-sided, lovable genius. The Thurber work is not only first-rate journalism (and to Thurber and a few more of us that is high praise) but, unless I am greatly in error, it is magnificent history and will be read with delight and wonderment for decades. We have had nothing quite like it. And Thurber, great man though he is, never wrote anything better. Good for him, and good for *The Atlantic*.

Yours,

STANLEY WALKER

P.S. I guess, in the long gunsight of history, you were lucky. What has happened to New York, and particularly to my old paper, makes me terribly sad, and I had hoped not to be sad as I entered old age.

---

1. While Walker was with *The New Yorker*.

LAST LETTERS
TO THE WHITES

From their initial meeting in 1927 to Thurber's death in the fall of 1961, Andy White was the friend he depended on, whose approval he sought, from whom, as he said, he "learned more about writing than from anybody else."

A temporary rift developed in 1958 while Thurber was writing The Years with Ross, which became a best-seller. The Whites, with others at The New Yorker, thought the book intrusive and indelicate, but Andy and Katharine in time got over their pique.

Time *was researching its cover story on Thurber and these were some of the preliminaries.*

◄-◄►►

West Cornwall,
Connecticut
July 19, 1950

Dear Infielders:

A dozen of my friends have been trying to handle those queerly bouncing balls for the past two weeks. My mother and brothers had to deal with a man from *Time*'s staff in Washington, D.C., who flew out. "He was born on August eighth," she told me later on the phone.[1] They drove him to see all the houses we have lived in, my grandfather's store, and the rifle range where Dr. James E. Snook killed Theora Hix. They hit Honey[2] with "Does he have compassion?" She chose to reply by telling how I had taken her apartment to pieces and lied about my having thrown a box of candy. McNulty said, "I told them everything except how Jimmy held the ladder for Hauptmann,"[3] they got twenty pages of notes from Ronnie and Janey Williams, and I haven't heard from Elliott, who was cornered in Hollywood. The man they sent to call on Althea acted subdued in Dr. Gilmore's house,[4] since he was the education editor of the *Pittsburgh Press,* as well as the *Time* man. He kept swallowing a lot, but Althea phoned me that she came out of it all right but was unable to tell what streets we lived on in Columbus and when I first became interested in dogs, since she wasn't born then. The prize question knocked at me was "Do you consider yourself complex?"

We all wonder what becomes of *Time* men and women after the age of thirty. McNulty said that his man hadn't heard of Frank Tin-

1. Thurber's mother was an avid astrology enthusiast.
2. Ann Honeycutt, Thurber's early flame.
3. Bruno Richard Hauptmann kidnapped and killed the Lindbergh baby.
4. Thurber's first wife had married a history professor named Allan Gilmore.

ney,[5] Honey said they couldn't identify anybody before 1928, and Althea reported that her man seemed to regard her as being a contemporary of the late Evangeline Booth.[6] The man who called on me is writing the piece and was six years old when I went to work on *The New Yorker*. The girl researcher with him was two at that time. They cabled T. S. Eliot after talking to Pete De Vries, said that their dinner with Ross gave them nothing since he can't remember anything, but Lobrano, like the others, found these two smart, friendly, and hardworking. I tried to keep *Time* from tracking you down on vacation, but they love it when it's hard. This cover story originated when we met Tom Matthews at Kenyon, and we liked each other and are spending a weekend with him in August. He is a fine man and is responsible, I think, for *Time*'s mature and unmalicious cover stories, such as the one on Eliot.

I found out a lot about myself in listening to my friends' accounts of what they wouldn't tell. Ross wouldn't tell a remark of Gibbs's that I hadn't known: "He's the nicest guy in the world until five P.M." I passed it on to *Time* myself, together with Althea's "You're not a bad boy trying to be good, you're a good boy trying to be bad." I told them I had been trying to overcome a stubborn defense mechanism that has operated after five P.M. and was so frank in this regard that they seemed to think I was intent on setting this tone. God knows how the piece will come out, but I hope no one else but me is hit. They have promised to omit the Stanley Walker story of the divorce in the *Mirror*, which they had dug up along with themes of mine in the fifth grade. Janey Williams said she never saw me throw anything at a girl and the piece may finally end up as a comparative study of female targets. . . .

Love and kisses from Helen and Rosie and me.

As ever,

JIM . . .

5. The deceased vaudevillian.
6. Leader of the Salvation Army.

◄◄►►

West Cornwall,
Connecticut
October 5, 1950

Dear Andy:

The *Time* piece, as written by the solemn man who was six when I went to work on *The New Yorker*, who first found out in July that I write and draw, and who for years has been a disciple of Whittaker Chambers, was as great a mess as you would want to see. Of seventy-three facts, only nineteen were right, and all I learned about myself was that I have apparently not got a thickening of the capsule of the lens, but a carapace of glaucoma, or so the piece says. This is a little like finding out that the injury you suffered in the Cornell–Pennsylvania game was actually syphilis.

Matthews had thought of Sayre as well as you — confidentially, a breath after he thought of you — and Joe may take on the piece, since he has got out from under his television stint, which he always calls "the garbage." I had told the *Time* man so many of the dark things about me that this confession became known at *Time*, and when I told Matthews I could write the article myself, he said, "We don't want an unfriendly piece." There was also some feeling that, in a later mood, I might sue myself.

The material on me, much of it gleaned from friends between midnight and morning, was so extensive that the writer couldn't find anything he was looking for, and, with data up to his waist, had to guess and make things up. He insisted that the one drawing he liked and the one fable were "the famous ones," which gave me practically nothing to sustain my vanity. . . .

Love and kisses to you and Kay from Helen and me,

As always,

JIM

➤◄◇►

The Ledgelets
Somerset Bridge,
Bermuda
April 24, 1951

Dear Andy:

Helen read me your "Two Letters," and I felt, as I always do when one of your too rare things like it appears, that you ought to do more. It is a beauty, and nobody else could come close to writing like that. I think you probably have the wrong idea about humor in our time, which I gather from the Kramer book[1] and other sources. Every time is a time for humor, especially now, because the Communists set out long ago to knock it off, and writing it is doing battle in one small corner of the field. They have tried to destroy racial humor, and have put up quite a campaign against comedy about Jews or colored people, so that what is left is usually pretty heavy and exaggerated, and they ignore the fact that the best Jewish and colored stories are told by Jews and colored people. Twelve years ago, Donald Stewart debated Benchley on the subject "Shall There Be Humor about the Working Classes?," and the leftist, of course, took the negative.

It is certainly not easy to write humor now, but that is one of the challenges. You are more serious than humorous, by choice, whereas I am the other way round, by circumstance. If the good century ever arrives, the humor you write is likely to survive as well as the serious stuff, and some of it more so, because much of the serious stuff will come out as timely and topical. Old Santayana went right on with philosophy in Italy during the war, paying no attention to the rumble of momentary history outside his windows.

I write humor the way a surgeon operates, because it is a livelihood, because I have a great urge to do it, because many interesting challenges are set up, and because I have the hope that it may do some good. When the leftists got hold of Dorothy Parker, they persuaded her to say in *The New Masses*, "Humor is a shield and not

1. *Ross and The New Yorker* by Dale Kramer.

a weapon." It is both and neither, but I remember how, at one battle in Gaul, members of the Tenth Legion banged the bejesus out of the enemy with their shields when their swords were gone. This piece of yours proves again that you can do it better than anybody, and I don't like to have the Communists gloating over the retirement of any humorist, even if they don't manage it by direct onslaught. . . .

Love and kisses to you from Helen and me,

As always,

JIM . . .

-◄-◇-►-

West Cornwall,
Connecticut
December 22, 1952

Dear Andy:

Everybody but me among us old codgers proudly insists that he and his wife were married just like the kids of today, without a blinking cent or the hope of work, and this is simply a lot of whoosh. After you had made the same boast, I sat around figuring that you and Katharine had made, together, a cool $20,800 in 1928, before there were any taxes to speak of. Like me, you would have dropped dead before asking a girl to marry you while you were still in college and had nothing to offer but a room in the Phi Gam House, which you shared with brother Kilroy.

Rosie's future father-in-law[1] is Park Commissioner of Chicago, I think, and a *Who's Who* landscape architect who has been past president of all their organizations. He is a Purdue man, two years older than me. (It's not easy to make *Who's Who,* since Red Grange couldn't do it and he's one of the ten best-known men in America.) What scalds us fathers of the brides is that the fathers of the sons seem to put it all on us, beginning with the wedding reception, at which we buy all the liquor and they don't even set up one round. . . .

If I had married Minnette Fritts when I was at Ohio State, we would have had thirty-five cents a day, and the astonishment of it all would have killed my father. I can also see yours, an outstandingly orderly man with a love of the hardworking ball bearing, saying to your mother about 1920, "I have just learned that Andy has married a Kappa Kappa Gamma sophomore at Cornell. Do you know precisely what this means?"

It is the women who love the insecurity before they are thirty. Althea forced me to give up my good paying jobs in Columbus and sail for France. A year later I borrowed $300 from Red Morrison,[2] by collect cable from Villefranche, and six months after that I bor-

---

1. Charles Goodwin Sauers.
2. A friend from Columbus.

rowed a few hundred francs on my return ticket on the *Leviathan*, hating every part of it. We owed a Left Bank hotel a couple of hundred francs when I got a check for $90 from "*Harper's* Lion's Mouth." This made us violently rich and is the most financial fun I ever had, even counting the $3,000 I kept out of my check for $40,000 from the Book-of-the-Month Club, to buy Helen a mink coat. The other $37,000, with $27,000 added to it, went to the U.S. Treasury. They wanted $17,000 more on this same deal a few years ago, but Helen won a long and adroit battle with the tax court. The poverty-stricken bridegrooms will never get into this, anyway.

Said our milkman the other day, "My nephew Joe has a baby at the Harvard Law School." . . . Manic depression among young men at college is on the increase. Their brides will see them through, however, just as yours and mine have seen us through. I know that Katharine would slop the pigs for you in a crisis, even if she were wearing an evening dress and silver dancing slippers.

Merry Christmas to you and Katharine and Joe, and all your other loved ones from all of us.

As always,

POOR OLD,

JT

P.S. When I married Helen I had three pints of rye and no money, and owed $2,500. But I had proved I could make money if I put my mind to it and quit sitting around thinking up new ways to kill Ann Honeycutt. She told Helen the other day that she had finally decided I didn't like her. She is right and I have figured out why. Our love never ripened into friendship. . . .

◄-◄◇-►

West Cornwall,
Connecticut
February 20, 1954

Dear Andy:

I know you will want to read the Davis[1] letter, so here it is. His wartime job also gave him important experience and we don't have to worry about anything happening to him politically. His trouble is mainly blood pressure. He has learned to bear up under McCarthy pressure. His courage under any pressure is heartening for all of us. I knew that he had been depressed by having to give up his daily work and I knew, as I told you, that sending the proof would mean quite a lot to him, as this letter proves. You can return it when you want to, since I keep his letters. Why don't you arrange to have lunch with him at the Algonquin some Saturday. I know he would love it. . . .

I hope Katharine's mumps and your shingles will soon be things of the forgotten past. I was depressed by a lot of things when I phoned you and my statistics are those of a man who will soon be sixty, not a youngster like you. Yours is the type of human physique that goes on forever. I have a way of counting my dead friends and former colleagues like beads, but I have decided to give it up. Most of them were guys of heavy torso and big bellies and bottoms.

The success of your book[2] is one of the cheerful things of the decade. Love and kisses to you and Katharine.

As ever,

JIM

P.S. Since Helen's bad siege at the hospital, and even before, I have been owing and writing letters to the sick and disabled and down, in hospitals and out, because I realize the tremendously good effect on morale that this has. If I had not sent the proof, you would not

1. Broadcaster Elmer Davis, who had served as director of the Office of War Information.
2. White's collection *The Second Tree from the Corner.*

be able to read such a letter as this one from Davis, so once in a while transgressions of rules are on the side of the angels. I read a garble not long ago for "angle of repose" which came out angel of repose, a mighty good angel to have around these days. Angle of repose is usually applied to an angle that will let go at the slightest disturbance, causing landslides, filling up Culebra Cut, and making it necessary to start work all over again. The angel of repose, on the other hand, keeps the balance secure with nothing more than a cheerful word or an unauthorized proof sent through the mails. . . . As you and I know, H. W. Ross had dealings with the angel of repose and was good at the cheerful word of praise. . . .

I'm accumulating some clips to send to you when I get them all together, one of them from a Baltimore paper quoting part of your preface to *Is Sex Necessary?* — the wonderful paragraphs dealing with the fact that aviation had to be made safer to attract people, just as sex had to be made more complicated and dangerous. Nobody but you could have put this in the exactly right words, which I am not attempting.

Love,

JIM

◄◄►►

West Cornwall,
Connecticut
April 9, 1954

Dear old White:

I'm glad you got the book award from the Newspaper Guild. How's about writing Brownell[1] and asking him to put on the subversive list all the organizations that have honored McCarthy with a good-citizenship award? Elliott says an FBI man called on him some weeks ago as part of a field investigation of Robert Montgomery. This, sir, is the quintessence of supersecurity. Helen and I had a few drinks with Elmer Davis at the Algonquin. He remembered Ross's showing him a cheque for $1,000 back around 1927

and saying, "This is the biggest cheque we've ever sent out or ever will send out." It was made out to John Winkler and was payment for five pieces on J. P. Morgan or John D. Rockefeller. Boy, the rooking everybody took in those days from a magazine that didn't know its own financial strength. Ross was thrown off by the fact that you and I got paid for other things than casuals, like Talk, Comment,

1. Herbert Brownell, U.S. attorney general.

drawings, captions, etc., and it wasn't until 1941 or thereabouts, after Perelman and Sullivan had complained to me that they couldn't afford to write casuals for *The New Yorker* to the limit of their ability, and after I had told Ross that a humorist turning out twelve pieces a year would make about $3,500 at best, that he said, "Jesus Christ, I never thought of it that way," and word rates were jumped from 200 percent to 300 percent. You were known in those days as the boy who thought he was getting plenty, didn't want a raise, and once tore up a cheque and sent back the pieces. How did I get into this? I started this letter to suggest a pamphlet by you entitled "Thirty Interesting Ways to Warm Over Spaghetti," or "How to Heat Spaghetti Without Cooking the Rye." . . .

As ever,

Jɪᴍ

◄◄►►

West Cornwall,
Connecticut
June 30, 1954

Dear Andy:

. . . Helen and I are in fine fetlock and feather after our stay in Bermuda. Ada's lawn has developed ants of two varieties, one of which nips. The mullet still leap out of the water in the inlet behind Waterville, after sundown, but she still hasn't found out why. At first I figured they were like Ed Wynn's horse that kept bumping into things: "He isn't blind, he just doesn't give a good goddamn," but then a better explanation occurred to me: the leaping fish are males whose exasperated wives have said, "Ah, go jump out of the lake!" . . .

We hope you and Katharine are okay. Don't write and edit yourselves into premature old age. I am writing what looks like a series of three or more pieces about Ross. Fadiman[1] said the other night on a premiere of a radio program called "Conversation," which discussed great talkers, including Ross, that the latter was unpredictable. I have given this much thought, but still insist that I rarely found him unpredictable. I was often in the middle of a sentence before he had started it. I am using a lot of quotes from him, since I remember thousands, including "Mrs. Angell knows the Bible and foreign languages and has taste." Also how he once said to her, "Now Thurber is playing with dolls," and, on another occasion, "Thurber was at Tony's with an *actress* last night," after which he put on that massive dejected look of his and asked plaintively, "Is Thurber attractive to *women?*" Your wife certainly had to deal with a lot of answers to hard questions.

Only story I picked up in Bermuda goes like this: Guy snarls at bartender, "I want something tall and cold and full of gin." Drunk at the end of the bar says, "You leave my wife out of this."

I am doing "Glimpses of Harold Ross" in kind of Talk of the Town style, chasing him casually from memory to memory, dealing

---

1. Clifton Fadiman, literary critic and radio emcee, formerly *The New Yorker*'s book reviewer.

with all his facets and maggots and prejudices, his perception, intuition, and plain ignorance, as they occur to me.

Did you ever hear Bob Coates's story about one Aaron Glemby, one of the three eccentric brothers who manufactured Venida hairnets? Aaron was on a subway train in New York when a fuse blew and he spotted smoke. He stood up on his seat and bawled, "Keep calm, everybody!" This started a panic. Finally a trainman appeared and bawled over the shouting and the turmoil, "Why doesn't somebody conk that son-of-a-bitch before we all get trampled to death?" This wonderful query could be applied to so many people today. . . .

Love and kisses,

As ever,

JIM

West Cornwall,
Connecticut
April 7, 1958

Dear Whites:

Thanks, Kitty, for your good letter on that big fat flounce, Woollcott. His last Shouts and Murmurs ran in the issue of December 29, 1934. He died, I think, about January 1943. I'm just finishing piece number nine, about him and Ross. I had intended to get in other stuff about Ross the Wag, too, but I can't do that terrible friendship under seven thousand words. Ross was just as bastardly to him as he was bitchy to Ross. The main difference was, seems to me, Woollcott's malevolence was mature, whereas Ross's long practical jokes were often childish, mischievous, and even cheap in the manner of Peck's Bad Boy. It's a savage and fascinating story, though, supplemented by quite a few letters and books. . . .

Andy's stuff on Ross and the automobile is simply superb. I can see them both on that goddam highway, and I wake up yelling,

"Look out!" When we do manage to get together, the four of us, you must read some other superb things that have been sent to me, letters from George Kaufman, O'Hara, Sam Behrman, Edmund Wilson, and Charles Cooke, with one from McKelway on its way. It's been held up by a train wreck near here which toppled freight cars and tore up a hundred yards of track.

A bachelor rabbit lives under our back porch, very lonely at Eastertime, I'll be bound, and the handsomest and sassiest male pheasant you ever saw walks around our front yard and driveway, prouder than a peacock and as bold as a hawk. We are also possum-bound, and if you ever stay here you can have possum for your breakfast when your sleepin' time is done. All the animals know we have no dog or cat and the master of the house can't see. . . .

As ever,

Jim

P.S. I fold copy paper all afternoon to cut down on smoking.

◄◄►►

West Cornwall,
Connecticut
June 2, 1958

Dear Andy and Katharine:

"Ross at the Wheel" is perfect.

One of my problems is dealing with his "Jesus" and "Christ" and "God damn," which I use that way only in what he himself or others have written, saying "Geezus" and "goddam" myself. I'll probably be excommunicated anyway.

Last Friday I lifted out the stuff on Ross's estate and the whole money business, not because I am all wet, but to put it in a folder called "Ross and Money."

I think you are a little damp yourselves about the payment setup, on which I am doing, and have done, immense and careful research, checking and double-checking. I held up my long letter to Hawley[1] until just now, because he won't get back from Europe until after I sail.

Among those who, in letters or in talks, agree with me about Ross and money are Ingersoll, Shuman, Bergman, Ralph Paladino, McKelway, Liebling, Mitchell, Cooke (who got $60 a week), Kinkead (who got $50), O'Hara, Sayre, Coates, to name a few. Liebling in his piece for me — "Impresario," and very fine it is, too — and Coates in his good piece both come out with the money thing. All the numerous quotes from all these people support me and, while I wait with honest eagerness and will use straight what Hawley has to say, I join all the others in believing, firmly, that neither Hawley nor any other editor exerted on Ross and Fleischmann[2] influence for fair pay, or, if they did, they got nowhere. The gentlest word about it all is "ridiculous," but "disgraceful" and "shameful" would not be too strong, nor would "idiotic." Eighty percent of the boys and girls use this line of Ross's, with variations — "We can't pay what is paid by *The Saturday Evening Post, Cosmopolitan, Life, Holiday, Ladies' Home Journal*, or *The Companion*" — and this line:

---

1. Hawley Truax, who for many years oversaw business matters at *The New Yorker*.
2. Raoul Fleischmann, owner and publisher of *The New Yorker*.

"*The New Yorker* is a showcase for authors." It was, too. Other magazines saw our work and paid us a decent amount, while Ross screamed and Fleischmann said, "This magazine will never pay a thousand dollars for a piece." Time proved he was wrong.

Ross's small, inexpert financial mind and his strange agonizing about it all were mainly responsible for the mess. After fourteen years on the magazine I didn't get decent money until *The Male Animal* and have nothing to show for pieces and drawings that fill twenty books. . . . I am, of course, not saying all of this, but treating it fairly and quietly. I once had to borrow $500 from the National City Bank with McKelway and Jap Gude going on my note. I had to borrow $2,500 from Elliott Nugent, and damn near left *The New Yorker* for Paramount Pictures in order to live. Liebling tells how he was in Ross's office one day and heard Ross say to the sick Gibbs on the phone, "Don't worry about money," and Joe had what he calls a "sibling feeling," for he has never got out of debt to the magazine. In Sayre's best year he wrote about eight casuals for us, for less than $3,000 in all, and had to write a book and go into the movies. . . . When I lay dying in Virginia in 1944, Helen wrote Ross for an advance against unused drawings of "Our New Natural History" and Ross wrote back his usual crap about "matter of bookkeeping" and "These things are not easy," and then in his famous P.S. in such matters said, "Don't worry about money." He was generous, but all balled up inside, and if Hawley can show me how he came to our rescue, I'll be God damned glad to read it and to use it.

This just scrapes the surface of it all. . . . If I ever write for *The*

New Yorker again, which I am afraid I doubt, I am going to hold the magazine to Lobrano's agreement. Nobody has done more for it than I have, even Andy, and I'm not going to be tortured by its pettiness and rule-bound cheapness. It can damn well pay what I deserve. For ten pieces in *The Atlantic* I was paid $15,000 and that magazine is poverty stricken compared to *The New Yorker*. I am not only one of our oldest contributors, but one of our saddest. *The New Yorker* supports Frank Adams,[3] but it will never support me. I am supported by book royalties from the publishers Ross said never paid writers.

With unshakable affection for both of you,

As always,

Jɪм

3. Franklin P. Adams (known as "F.P.A."), newspaper columnist, author, and radio panelist.

◄◄◇►

Ye Olde Bell
Hurley
Berkshire, England
August 7, 1958

Dear Andy and Katharine:

I am finishing the final five pieces of the Ross book over here, working day and night. The book has had to be put off until spring, because I refused to jam it through, and insisted on getting it right.

The fifteen chapters, supplemented with the wonderful stuff in End Papers, form a true biography of Ross and, I think, a sincere and complete history of *The New Yorker* — as well as that incredibly difficult task can be done. I keep getting wonderful letters, from Charles Addams, Shirley Jackson, the Marx brothers — really funny stuff — and others, including Stephen Botsford,[1] whom I like. My letters to him and to Raoul and to Hawley have all been straightforward, and so have their answers to them. The chapter called "The Dough and the System" now consists, in large part, of Ross's letters to me about money, which he always called dough, and my letters to him. Thus no one can question the authenticity of what each of us believed, whether it was right or wrong. Katharine and Ross and Lobrano and all the others delegated portions of their problems, but I have had to deal, all by myself, with damn near every *New Yorker* editor, writer and artist of consequence, and it hasn't been easy. Bob Coates wrote me that the one piece he did for my book was a back-breaking and nerve-racking job. This leaves no words whatever for my ordeal.

In the chapter called "Crises and Contretemps"[2] I had to deal with all the major crises, personal and legal and intramural, and it stands up as both sound and funny, I think, which is what I have been striving for. I try to tell every story and anecdote as fairly as possible, naturally leaving out a lot of stuff I would have liked to put in, leaving it out on behalf of *The New Yorker* people's famous sensitivity, discretion, and addiction to secrecy.

1. Raoul Fleischmann's stepson.
2. Retitled "Up Popped the Devil" before publication.

Raoul had told me, quite frankly, in answer to my direct questions, how he offered you two the joint job of editor in 1938, and I don't dwell on that but I have to put it down, or the book would be incomplete, untrue, and evasive. I should like to send you, when I get it rewritten the way I want it, a carbon of the paragraph or two about this. I consider it a miracle of secrecy, and a triumph of tact and discretion, that you both got through that crisis so beautifully, with no broken bones, and no tears and blood in the corridors and offices. I didn't know about it and neither did McKelway or [Ik] Shuman, then Ross's managing editor and Miracle Man respectively. McKelway, you know, signed a three-year contract in 1937 as managing editor (I have to use that term, for sanity's sake) at $15,000 a year, and Ik kept telling him he was in line for Ross's job. But that is, as you know, a long and tangled story, and I touch on it lightly, since McKelway was a writer anyway, and not an editor, really, and since he had, like most all the rest of us, his own cycle of ups and downs that dismayed Ross, almost as much as Lobrano's ups and downs.

It now turns out that I have more than a hundred letters from Ross written to me between 1944 and a few months before he died, and they form, usually in part, sometimes in their entirety, much of the bones of the remaining pieces.

I am saying, as of now anyway, that Ross never knew of Fleischmann's offer of his job to you. Again let me say I think this was handled wonderfully. I am not even saying that Andy began writing for *Harper's* in October 1938 and wrote "One Man's Meat" until 1943, during which time, or some of it, Gibbs did a lot of the Comment. I think we all believed that *The New Yorker* should always be edited by one person — Andy wrote that to me in Bermuda last spring — and that *The New Yorker* wouldn't be where it is today if Ross had not survived 1938 and been the man at the helm through the war years. That was when his great experience as a newspaperman was the quality most needed, but what he would have done without Shawn God only knows. I don't suppose Raoul had ever heard of William Shawn in 1938. Anyway, he had the good sense not to offer the job to anybody else after you turned it down.

I want to get through this book, which haunts my days and nights, without the loss of friends or weight or reason. I believe that nobody ever connected with *The New Yorker* can possibly have any sound objection to anything I have written or am writing for the book. I am using, in End Papers, the remarkable article from the *Wall Street Journal* of June 30, 1958. It sustains something I wrote a few weeks ago, before I saw the piece: "Fleischmann, it turned out, was not putting his money in jeopardy but in El Dorado, and what *The New Yorker* was slipping on, in the years when Ross was so sure it was slipping, was a bonanza peel." . . .

Love and kisses to you both, from Helen and me,

As ever,

JIM

P.S. I am also a little depressed by the silence of almost everybody on *The New Yorker*, except those in the business department. We have not heard from Miss Terry at all, and worry about it, and Hawley has not answered a few queries of mine, and nobody but you has written about the last *Atlantic* piece, but I did hear from Groucho Marx about it, and Nunnally[3] and a great many other friends and a great many strangers. Never in my whole life on *The New Yorker* have I got such letters as those that keep coming in from all over the world about the *Atlantic* pieces, from doctors, English professors, old ladies, and all sorts and conditions of both sexes. There is a good one from John Fischer of *Harper's*, too.[4] It certainly warms the blood and lifts the heart. . . .

3. Screenwriter Nunnally Johnson, an old colleague from Thurber's days on the *New York Evening Post*.
4. Fischer, editor of *Harper's*, was yet another *New Yorker* contributor.

◄◄►►

Hôtel Continental
Paris, France
October 22, 1958

Dear Whites:

. . . It is true that I have been, in part, crosshatching, but I am now restoring the simple form of the book, the familiar line. This takes out of the book some fifteen thousand words, but improves it. There was a sincere and sound unanimity of opinion from half a dozen persons, including you, that I had strayed from the course I had set. This had threatened *The Thurber Album*, too, but I managed to make it straighten out and fly right. I think I always do that in the end, but the straightening is something I have to see clearly myself before I can handle it. Black Velvet is not for me. Make mine Château d'Yquem, which, like my work, serves two purposes. It brightens children's birthday parties, not an easy thing to do when all the children want to bash each other with iron locomotives, and it is a solace to old ladies living in dread of the police finding the hiding places of their poisoned husbands. This is a small but friendly service, and we must all stay within our circumscribed areas of ability. We all want to play Hamlet, even those of us who are much better at Jeeter Lester. Let those who live in Frederick Street, or Peyton Place, write about it. I live in a land where a nightingale is singing and a white moon beams, and a man's heart, to paraphrase E. B. White, gets caught in an embrace when his foot is caught in a piano stool. You must remember Scaramouche, who was born with a gift of laughter and a sense that the world is mad.

One critic, back home, who has read the so-called completed manuscript, said, "It is too long for its interest." I got mad and upset, and then realized he was right. The story of Harold Ross, *The New Yorker*, and me, is a mere footnote to the story of our time, and we might as well face the truth that to researchers of the future, poking about among the ruins of time, we shall all be tiny glitters. But then, so are diamonds. Somebody has just brought out a long, long biography of Paganini, who, as I said in a letter to Ted Weeks, had only three things that Ross didn't have — a violin, tuberculosis, and syphilis. I was wrong, he had four things: the other is im-mortality. Blessed are the meek.

Hardest of all to do was to take out the End Papers, which sets for me a new, tremendous problem and anxiety. I am using only one in the book now, Andy's piece about Ross at the wheel, for which I have a perfect place in the text. It will finish and round out one of the best new chapters, called "Ross, not Tobogganing," which deals with his activities out of the office. It will follow the funny story of Ross and me in Paris in 1938. I had my car in Paris then, but Ross would have none of Thurber at the wheel, and so we visited the old *Stars and Stripes* building by taxi. Ross upset the old concierge, who had never heard of him or of the *Stars and Stripes*, by shouting at him in English, of which the old man under-stood not a word. I then took over in my uneasy French — I always pronounce *la guerre* as if it were *la gare* — and the old man, I see now, must have thought I was telling him this: "This whole build-ing is one great big railway station, for they sell American news-papers." As I say in the piece, the poor fellow had always believed that something like Ross would happen to him, and here it was.

The book will come out *toujours gai* now, and almost all of the magazine's weaknesses, and those of its editors and writers, will be smoothed over, left out, but not prettified. Fifty years from now, though, my papers, as they call them, which I am leaving to Yale, will serve as the basis of a truly serious and important story of *The New Yorker*, and of the literary annals of the time, if anybody will then care a darn. We will then, all of us, be glitters in the past, but remember what Dylan Thomas said: "They shall have stars at their feet and at their elbows, and death shall have no dominion, and death shall have no dominion."

As for me, I have promises to keep, and miles to go before I sleep, and miles to go before I sleep.

Knowing happily and full well that you have the same, I remain always,

Yours, with love and kisses,

Jim . . .

The Bawling Out

◄◄◊►►

West Cornwall,
Connecticut
November 21, 1958

Dear Andy:

I worry about your pukin' spells, so let me hear about you.

I have rewritten and cut the six new chapters so they conform in tone and shape with the others. You helped a lot, more than anyone, as always, when you warned me against crosshatching. I listened impatiently to the criticisms of Weeks, Morton, Fadiman, and John Mason Brown, but they were right. I have to see things finally for myself, which I usually do. Every long writing project of mine has been saved finally by my unconscious, the soundest critic I know. A week ago I dreamed I was sitting on a curb and picked up a muddy thing the shape of a gibbous croquet ball. When I got the mud off, there was a small clean crystal chalice. . . .

Ross is now quiet in heaven, I hope, and *The New Yorker* can breathe easier. My present dedication, a small but to me important one, is to prove to the *New Yorker* editors that I do, too, understand the psychology of a man of sixty. I am touching up that story for *The Atlantic,* since it is one of the best pieces I have ever written. The young *New Yorker* editors' odd belief that the story should have taken place ten years after the First World War, when my hero was only thirty, is, of course, in the American juvenile tradition that heros should never be forty, and heroines should be forever panting and forever twenty-three. My chief nightmares are still about Gus Kuehner,[1] my tough city editor of thirty-eight years ago. The return to ancient scenes, youthful scenes, of a man of sixty, is a common and fascinating phenomenon. Anyone who would let himself, at my age, keep on getting mad at *The New Yorker* would prove only that he is silly. Imagine, though, being buried between black borders under 248 pages of prose and advertising! Let us, for God sake, not die in November. I can't stand the thought of a 200-pound

1. Norman "Gus" Kuehner, of the *Columbus Dispatch.*

dowager with 48 pounds of gaudy jewelry lying upon my dead body.

I have rededicated my book to Frank Sullivan, instead of Alva Johnston, on the principle of Flowers for the Living. I phoned Frank about it this morning and it was a joy to hear the light in his voice. . . .

Love,

JIM

◄◇►

West Cornwall,
Connecticut
July 9, 1959

Dear Andy:

Thought you would be interested in the enclosed letter from
Charles Brackett[1] and the Muggeridge[2] review from *The New States-
man* of London. You all can send them back when you finish them.
I have material enough for a future historian in letters from men
like Elmer Adler, aged seventy-five, who helped design *The New
Yorker* and, for pay, got a life subscription. . . .

The chill, clamlike silence of most *New Yorker* people has been
burned away by the great warm reception of the book all over the
civilized world. Nobody, but nobody, outside 25 West 43rd and
environs, sees in it anything but a warm, affectionate tribute to
H.W.R. Best letter, and one of very few from present *New Yorkers*,
came from Edmund Wilson, signed "With much enthusiasm."
Tynan's review in the *London Observer* remarkably shows how
quickly an outsider becomes somaticized on the weekly. It is post-
collaborative and a curious self-revelation, but the few adverse reviews are in some ways the most interesting or fascinating, such as
Dawn Powell's strange document, and David Cort's even stranger
one in *The Nation.* He likes me and the book, but God how he hated
Ross! Rebecca West has done the book for the *London Sunday Times*,
but I haven't got it yet.

One famous writer asked me, "Do you realize your book is autobiographical?" Good God, it must be the fallout. What could be
more studiedly autobiographical than the title itself. Many have
read the book without reading it. I say in it, "one man's opinion,
personal and debatable." The mortal enemy of the present *New
Yorker* is smallness, which must never be confused with Size. *Time*
is doing the fine Strunk–White book,[3] which I am just starting. A

1. The screenwriter and producer, former drama critic for *The New Yorker.*
2. Malcolm Muggeridge, former editor of *Punch.*
3. *The Elements of Style,* by William Strunk, Jr., which White revised.

Time gal phoned me to see if I still stuck to a quote of mine she found in the *Time* clips: "I learned more about writing from White than from anybody else," said humorist James Thurber. I told her I sure did stick to it. . . .

As ever,

JIM

◄◄►►

West Cornwall,
Connecticut
July 12, 1961

Dear old Andy:

When you die and I die we won't need to have any bull killed. In our time we have killed as much bull as any two guys anybody can name.

I keep monkeying with a piece about my various hospitalizations, which began at the Garfield Hospital in Washington, D.C., the month you and Hemingway became two years old. Then, and ever since then, all my doctors have marked my chart "atypical." It turned out, at the C&O Hospital in Clifton Forge, Virginia, in 1944, that my appendix, which was retrocecal, had probably been gangrenous for months, without pain. When it ruptured one day at six A.M. there was no pain and I was hungry! I had no nausea. A puzzled surgeon down there telephoned my surgeon at Medical Center, who said, "That's Thurber all right. You'd better operate." But the surgeon who performed the operation was out quail hunting and fifteen hours went by before the operation. The doc told Helen that she'd better be on call that night. I was fed intravenously for more than two weeks and in the hospital for a month. When I conquered the peritonitis and at last got up and dressed, the surgeon said, "How do you account for your resilience?" I told him about my mother's family and he said, "That's it." Three women lived to be more than a hundred, and many others, including men, got in their nineties. Genes, enzymes, and all that. One reason I want to write the piece is to show how the incurable do recover — fifty-four cases in the last twelve years of men and women recovering from the tertiary stage of what Nunnally Johnson calls "the stuff." The doctors tell me that all they have to do now is to find out what the body knows that they don't know, and the stuff will be easy to manage. One man who was given sixty days to live popped into his doctor's office a year later, completely cured, and the doctor fainted. The "dead" man managed to get him to a couch.

My strangest atypicality, of course, is the demonstrable fact that

I lost the sight of both eyes in 1902, but could see "without the apparatus of vision" for thirty-eight years. "I can't believe God wanted you to do those drawings," said Dr. Bruce, but I told him I could.

Let us then be up and doing, with a heart for any fate.

Once again, our love and best wishes to Katharine and you.

As ever,

JIM

THE
NEW YORKER'S
FAREWELL

Written by William Shawn and E. B. White, The New Yorker's *parting tribute was published November 11, 1961.*

James Thurber

James Thurber, who died on November 2, 1961, at the age of sixty-six, added more than one man's share to the world's small store of humor and wisdom. In a lifelong act of generosity, he poured out his hundreds upon hundreds of drawings, stories, fables, memoirs, and essays — many of them among the funniest any writer or artist has ever produced — and turned them over to us in the warranted expectation that they would make us laugh, instruct us, shake us up, and keep us going. His work was largely unclassifiable (it was simply Thurber), and by the end it gave him a place in history as one of the great comic artists and one of the great American humorists. *The New Yorker* was privileged to be Thurber's home base. From 1927, two years after the magazine began, until 1933, he was on the editorial staff, contributing not only his writings and drawings but also his exhilarating presence. In the early days, when the magazine was first being formed, he was one of those who helped form it. His tremendously original point of view, his literary style, his peculiar kind of vigor and restlessness all went into the magazine and became a part of its tradition. He was one of the early writers of the Talk of the Town, and, in a sense, was one of its inventors. His influence on the magazine was lasting. Certainly there will never be an issue of *The New Yorker* of which Thurber is not a part. After he left the staff, he continued to contribute his writing and his art, and he contributed until the time of his death. Today, even the sound of his titles can be stirring: "The Secret Life of Walter Mitty," "The Departure of Emma Inch," "The Night the Bed Fell," "The Unicorn in the Garden," and on and on. Those of us who were his colleagues feel that on Thurber one man in particular can and should speak for us all, and that is E. B. White, so the words that follow are his:

I am one of the lucky ones; I knew him before blindness hit him, before fame hit him, and I tend always to think of him as a young artist in a small office in a big city, with all the world still ahead. It was a fine thing to be young and at work in New York for a new magazine when Thurber was young and at work, and I will always be glad that this happened to me.

It was fortunate that we got on well; the office we shared was the size of a hall bedroom. There was just room enough for two men, two typewriters, and a stack of copy paper. The copy paper disappeared at a scandalous rate — not because our production was high (although it was) but because Thurber used copy paper as the natural receptacle for discarded sorrows, immediate joys, stale dreams, golden prophecies, and messages of good cheer to the outside world and to fellow workers. His mind was never at rest, and his pencil was connected to his mind by the best conductive tissue I have ever seen in action. The whole world knows what a funny man he was, but you had to sit next to him day after day to understand the extravagance of his clowning, the wildness and subtlety of his thinking, and the intensity of his interest in others and his sympathy for their dilemmas — dilemmas that he instantly enlarged, put in focus, and made immortal, just as he enlarged and made immortal the strange goings-on in the Ohio home of his boyhood. His waking dreams and his sleeping dreams commingled shamelessly and uproariously. Ohio was never far from his thoughts, and when he received a medal from his home state in 1953, he wrote, "The clocks that strike in my dreams are often the clocks of Columbus." It is a beautiful sentence and a revealing one.

He was both a practitioner of humor and a defender of it. The day he died, I came on a letter from him, dictated to a secretary and signed in pencil with his sightless and enormous "Jim." "Every time is a time for humor," he wrote. "I write humor the way a surgeon operates, because it is a livelihood, because I have a great urge to do it, because many interesting challenges are set up, and because I have the hope it may do some good." Once, I remember, he heard someone say that humor is a shield, not a sword, and it made him mad. He wasn't going to have anyone beating his sword into a shield. That "surgeon," incidentally, is pure Mitty. During his happiest years, Thurber did not write the way a surgeon operates, he wrote the way a child skips rope, the way a mouse waltzes.

Although he is best known for "Walter Mitty" and *The Male An-*

imal, the book of his I like best is *The Last Flower.* In it you will find his faith in the renewal of life, his feeling for the beauty and fragility of life on earth. Like all good writers, he fashioned his own best obituary notice. Nobody else can add to the record, much as he might like to. And of all the flowers, real and figurative, that will find their way to Thurber's last resting place, the one that will remain fresh and wiltproof is the little flower he himself drew, on the last page of that lovely book.

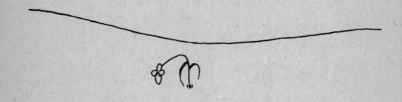

Index